Molluscs

M and

Helen Howard

MOLLUSCS AND ME

is published by

H&RH Escargots
18 St Vincents Close, Littlebourne
Canterbury, Kent CT3 1TZ

www.hrh-escargots.co.uk

First published in Great Britain 2013

By the same author:
Smallholder Guide to Farming Edible Snails
(available from H&RH Escargots)

Other writing by the same author on health and
social care, regulation and management has been
published by Anglia Ruskin University, the Open
University, the former Age Concern (England), the
National Extension College, the Open Learning
Foundation and Scitech Educational Ltd.

The story told in this book is based on real events
but the names of people involved have been changed to
protect their identity.

Contents

Foreword

Helen Howard has been a producer member of Produced in Kent since 2008 and I can recall being utterly amazed at her new enterprise when we first met. Cultivating snails for the retail and hospitality sectors, effectively a mass market, was entirely new to me and yet I was intrigued to know more and sat down eagerly in her small house near Canterbury to find out all about it. She is unique to Kent but I have since learned that there are other snail farmers – and that's what Helen is – around the country.

Helen has doggedly retained an entrepreneurial spirit since setting up this business and has diversified into a variety of ways in which to educate and inform us mere mortals in the way of the snail! She engages wonderfully with young children and adults alike.

As a small business Helen approached Produced in Kent, a local food promotion group in Kent, for help and support. The challenges of refining the product, packaging, finding new opportunities and routes to market are the same faced by many small food businesses. Whilst Produced in Kent has provided some of these opportunities, Helen has in reality done most of the work herself and this book sets out to demonstrate her journey. It will prove to be an interesting read, taking the reader to many and varied places never visited before and with snails for company.

I wish Helen every success, not only with this unique book, but with the snails and her work in the future.

Stephanie Durling
On behalf of the team at Produced in Kent

Prologue

'This week's edition of Countryfile comes to you from the garden of England.' Julia Bradbury looked around and the camera showed her walking along an ordinary street of 1950s semi-detached and terraced houses. 'So you must be wondering what I'm doing here.' She stopped outside my house and looked quizzically into the camera. 'I think you will be quite surprised by what's happening behind this modest front door.'

I held my breath, feeling my heart beat as I waited for her knock.

The houses were built at a time when it was understood that people who lived on low incomes would need a patch of ground to grow their own food. It was always gardens that attracted me and this was no exception. This long narrow strip laid to grass with a concrete path and narrow border along one side was punctuated by the weeping branches of a silver birch framing the view of fields beyond. It was a blank canvas on which I could paint my new life. I came to live here after my daughters had found their way in the world, when I emerged from a marriage that should have lasted forever but didn't. On a sunny day in June I moved my belongings in and began to make it home.

The kitchen stretched across the back of the house so

I could watch my garden grow through the patio doors and see next door's cat picking his way carefully across my view as I peeled vegetables at the sink. The sitting room was soon lined with bookshelves and my desk took up most of the rest of the space. I wasn't intending to put my feet up just yet. It was the first time I'd lived on my own since I was a student in a bedsit and the small house felt very spacious. There were two spare rooms to play with. I had my own space and I was determined to make the most of it.

As a child, I was pushed through the education system very fast, leaping over classes and taking exams early. But by seventeen, when I walked out of the school gates for the last time with plenty of exam results, I had learnt that ambition was not feminine and that girls should expect to take supporting roles or work in public service. We were certainly not prepared for leadership and I don't think the word 'entrepreneur' was in our vocabulary. It was ridiculously easy to find work when I was a teenager. I applied for seven jobs that fitted my qualifications, had three interviews and was able to choose which one I wanted. But after a couple of years of commuting to London to work in hospital research laboratories, I started to develop a bit of ambition and decided to go to university to study biological sciences.

Three years later, emerging as a newly qualified graduate, if there was one thing I didn't want to be, it was a teacher. But by then it was difficult to get anything else. Discrimination against women was rife. At interviews I was asked how long my soon-to-be husband was intending to stay in his job and when we planned to have children. One panel explained to me earnestly that the job they had advertised wouldn't be suitable for me because it wouldn't fit in with children. I would have to work from 8 until 5 and I wouldn't be able to take time off in the school holidays. More qualifications and advancing age seemed to have narrowed my options instead of expanding them and I found myself pushed into the school classroom as a teacher for a couple of mutually uncomfortable years. What the boys thought of my efforts to instil a little scientific method into their minds I have no idea, but for me it was a very unpleasant experience. They were ordinary teenagers who wrote rude words on the blackboard, brought me unknown creatures in matchboxes and tried to look up my skirt. It all sounds quite tame now but at the time it was more than I could deal with. After a couple of long years of torture and sleepless nights I found the entrance to the escape tunnel. My daughters arrived in my life not a moment too soon. While the girls were young, I patched together bits of part time and temporary work wherever I could get them. Most were related to education in some way, from running a literacy project to training preschool leaders, from making and selling children's dressing up clothes to managing a field study centre. As the girls grew up and my priorities changed, a full time job became an essential pre-requisite to getting a mortgage and becoming self-supporting. But now, in middle age, waiting for the TV cameras to roll through the front door, I felt as though my career proper was just beginning to get started.

1
A better way
of making a living

'I'm a farmer,' I said confidently, 'and these little darlings are my farm animals.' I opened the box on the table in front of me, picked up the slumbering snail and held it up on the flat of my hand. I'd picked a big one with a beautiful shell which shone brown and gold under the artificial lights. There was an audible intake of breath from the diners as the snail slowly uncurled its pale slender body, responding to the warmth of my hand. It explored my fingers gently and looked out over the edge of my palm, acknowledging the audience with a gracious bow. I had their attention at last.

I looked round the room at the tables littered with the remains of the worst meal I'd eaten since I left school: bland meat and vegetables microwaved to extinction. The air was stuffy, the walls faintly patterned in cream, the chandeliers dusty. A dozen grey men in their everyday suits, crumpled shirts and ties slumped at each table. They were beginning to relax, legs stretched out, stroking their wine glasses for comfort as they gazed into the middle distance. I could see their day to day experience reflected in their faces.

'Why snails?' asked the chairman encouragingly.

'As farm animals, snails have lots to recommend them. They don't bite or kick or make a noise and annoy the neighbours. They don't take up much space and they are really very accommodating. I can go away for a weekend and they just go to sleep and wait for breakfast to turn up.'

I paused for their response. It was a bit like doing a stand up routine - timing was everything. 'You don't have to use a dog to herd them from place to place or a lorry to get them to market and I can still run faster than they can.' They laughed.

'But I'm sure you'd all like to get a closer look at my business partners,' I said. I picked up the travelling boxes I'd brought and handed them round so each table had their own snail to make friends with. Predictably, their reactions varied from curiosity to horror.

'How did you get into the business?' called out one of the diners.

'I was downsized,' I said, indicating my small frame. 'I used to be six foot tall.' They laughed again and I looked around the room, wondering how they would react to the 'R' word. I side-stepped and I moved them seamlessly along to the next well-rehearsed anecdote, my mind elsewhere.

Redundancy was one of the best things that ever happened to me, but it took me a while to see it. The tension seemed to scramble my brain; I rushed about being busy but couldn't settle to anything. Working for a local authority was not the comfortable secure experience I'd imagined. My permanent post was deleted from the structure four times in the seven years I was there. If I took a holiday I could never be sure of finding my job still waiting on my return. It was like that for most of my colleagues too so when they asked for volunteers to be made redundant, thousands of hands shot up. The economy was apparently healthy so we had good reason to expect to find work outside. I'd had enough of working in a big organisation. I could let go of commuting and going to meetings held for the sake of having meetings. I couldn't wait to leave.

Getting rid of us was one thing Kent County Council did rather well. There was a good payoff and shedding the mortgage was wonderfully liberating. They nursed us tenderly out of the door with support and advice by the bucket-load. 'Managing Transitions' was what they called the programme for leavers. That's where I met Sarah. Memorable for her bright hair and round comforting shape, she was an outsider who filled the room with excitement, greeting us each time with a hug and bringing her knowledge and experience to share.

'When you work freelance, customers will be attracted not by what you know but by who you are. There may be lots of people who can do what you do but you have to persuade them to buy from *you*.' It was the first part of a crash course in marketing, which was something I'd only experienced from the receiving end. She assured us there was life outside KCC and she was right.

At not quite 50 I considered myself in the prime of my life, but I had to be realistic and accept that potential employers might not see it that way. Stability, it seemed, would only come from creating work for myself. By the time I left, I had two academic contracts to rely on to pay for my daily bread: some teaching and some writing. I soon settled down to the routine of working at home; switching on the computer as soon as I woke and starting to write with my breakfast bowl beside me. Books grew, chapter by chapter, and it wasn't long before they were ring-bound and in use as a source of study.

I did some teaching for the Open University, which was a revelation compared with school teaching, where I had never felt at home. Instead of having to control recalcitrant teenagers, here were adult students who wanted to be there and relished the opportunity for debate and discussion. They were mostly women trying to get better jobs or return to work after having children; some as old as me, bemoaning the way they'd wasted their opportunities when younger:

'I left school at fifteen with no qualifications... had a couple of kids and never really had what you'd call a career ... spent twenty years looking after them and my husband. Now they've all gone – including him – and I'm thinking, "What can I do with the rest of my life?"'

'You've come to the right place,' I said.

1a Introducing edible snails

Snails are molluscs, like cockles and mussels, oysters and winkles, the seafood that we're so familiar with. Slugs are also molluscs but snails and slugs are similar but different. When people ask me what the difference is I usually compare them with lions and tigers. They are both big cats so they are similar but you wouldn't mistake one for the other. So slugs and snails belong to the same group of animals – the gastropods – but they are different. Most of the slugs you come across in the garden don't have a visible shell. Snails usually have a coiled shell that they can retreat into. There are 124 different species of land snails in the British Isles (Cameron and Riley 2008) but most of us have probably only noticed three or four different kinds in our gardens. Most of these snails are edible but only a few are farmed for the table.

Helix aspersa (Cornu aspersum)

This species is the one referred to in Britain as the common garden snail. However, a number of sub species and varieties have been developed for farming to change the rate of growth, adult size and flavour of the meat. It is a very versatile species which can adapt to a range of climatic conditions and responds well to intensive farming conditions.

In France, Helix aspersa muller is called "petit-gris", which translates as the "little grey". The shell measures 18 - 32 mm in length and 20 – 40 mm diameter. It is widely eaten across Europe and the rest of the world.

Helix aspersa maxima is referred to as "gros-gris", which means "big grey", and it is the largest of the sub species, the shell diameter measuring 45 – 47 mm. A breeding population of this species can lay eggs all year round if kept under the right conditions. Each individual snail, however, may only lay eggs once or twice before dying. Because of its adaptability it is farmed in many different countries around the world.

2
Chelsea Flower Show

It was time for a mother and daughter day out and neither of us had ever been to the Chelsea Flower Show. For Rebecca weekends were for riding. She lived in the wilds of the West Midlands, and living so far apart and leading such busy lives meant we didn't meet very often. Standing on Euston station waiting for her train to come in it wasn't easy to see her slight figure in such a crowd. But eventually I spotted her long fair hair and waved to catch her attention. Since leaving agricultural college Rebecca had settled into an office job in Birmingham but she still felt the call of the outdoors. She rarely visited London so wasn't confident about finding her way around. The underground system was familiar to me from the days when I commuted to work in the research labs at St Mary's Hospital.

When we emerged from the station forecourt the sun was already warm although it was still early in the year. We got on the special bus to Chelsea and began to catch the atmosphere. The bus was full of summer dresses, smiling faces and excited anticipation.

My mother taught me all she knew about gardening. As a child she had wanted to be a scientist but her education was disrupted by moving to England from Wales when she was a teenager and there weren't the career opportunities for women then. But, like many parents, she was determined that I would achieve her dreams. As a child, every day was punctuated by time outside digging and planting, weeding and pruning. At the kitchen table we suffered cabbage with caterpillar, lettuce with slug and carrot with root fly. But the spiced pears or rhubarb crumble with custard and handfuls of soft fruit were a bonus worth waiting for. I had my own small plot from an early age after we moved out of London to the suburbs, so I was able to plant seeds and watch things grow.

On my bedroom window sill was a tank. It didn't have fish - just water, weed and snails with conical black shells. These water snails laid their eggs in jelly blobs on the sides of the aquarium and after a while tiny babies would emerge and crawl away across the glass. I remember spending hours in the long evenings watching them foraging through the water weed when I was supposed to be doing my homework.

My collection was there too: a bird skull and breastbone from the garden, a worn sheep's tooth from a Welsh hillside, fragments of blue sea glass, mussels and whelk shells, a mermaid's purse and a fossilised sea urchin from beach holidays, a green onyx egg from a white elephant stall and a tortoise ornament fashioned from a limpet shell with cockleshells for feet.

My garden is a bit rampant so it is no doubt full of slugs and snails. I tame it from time to time by going out with pruning shears and cutting back the worst of it, but you will always find more dandelions, daisies and clover in the lawn than grass and bindweed climbing every stem. A dead tree remains lying where it fell as a prop for pink clematis montana. My everlasting sweet-peas jump the fence and sun themselves on my neighbour's shrubs. The pond breeds frogs, mosquitoes and duckweed as well as those snails with sharply pointed shells, but no fish. Everything is planted close together and melts into a mass of pinks and blues. I won't have tropical invaders, only plants that have lived in Britain for a long time and flourish in the flinty clay soil. I've always liked growing things to eat: courgettes and tomatoes, spinach and French beans, parsley and coriander. Slug pellets have never appealed to me but I have to admit to setting beer traps and dropping the little beasts into salted water. Plums are a special treat so I have a damson and yellow plum but soft fruit too: blackcurrants, raspberries and alpine strawberries.

You can tell a lot about a person from their garden and if I meet someone who doesn't need one at all, I know we have nothing in common. The kind of garden I dislike is the one where bedding plants are replaced every year, sometimes more than once, to make a loud display that gets ripped out when it starts to fade. I like to see a garden develop over the years with plants that are meant to be permanent and prized for foliage and sculptural shape, not just flowers. Paths must meander and unexpected things allowed to happen.

The morning crowds at Chelsea drifted along the pathways between exhibits and stands and marquees. We learnt to avoid the knots of famous gardener groupies straining to catch every word the master said. They flowed around the grounds from one show garden to the next like swarms of bees around a queen.

At midday we sat on a low brick wall in the shade of a plane tree to eat sandwiches and talk about our hopes and dreams. It had taken me a long time to develop a sense of direction. Now Rebecca was struggling with her own career and lifestyle dilemmas. Perhaps many of us have dreams but haven't got the money to realise them. As I had no intention of making an early exit from this life I imagined my daughters being too old to enjoy their inheritance when it eventually came – perhaps just in time to pay their care home fees … if the money hadn't already gone paying mine. What I had, they needed now, while they were young and full of ideas. Rebecca's vision of the future had to involve horses.

When I was a child playing with my friends, we each

had our own imaginary herd of horses that we pretended to groom and ride. But the reality of riding was never a possibility so it soon faded and other games took its place. For Rebecca it was quite different. Her pleasure at being around horses easily became reality because we lived in a place where horses and ponies were part of the everyday scene. Riding wasn't an elite activity. Ponies were just part of the rural scene. Some of the older people who lived in the village had bought ponies for their offspring, now grown up, and they needed to be exercised. Many of the local children were able to take advantage of that opportunity without it costing them anything. Or they could go a step further and indulge their passion by having a pony on loan. Quite soon Rebecca was spending every spare moment at the local livery stables, which were within walking distance of our house. For a whole year she was there without pay every day before and after school and through the holidays mucking out the horses. There was no opportunity to ride the horses stabled there because she was inexperienced and still quite small in stature and they were too big and strong for her. I kept thinking she was going to get fed up with going out in all weathers to shovel manure with no reward but she didn't.

When Rebecca was thirteen we went to talk to the owner of the livery stables who agreed to help us find a suitable pony for her at a reasonable price and also agreed that she could keep it at the stables as long as she looked after it herself in return for helping out. My parents agreed to help with the purchase price and we found her a gymkhana pony called John Boy who was the perfect size and temperament. I can still remember taking her to a nearby village on her birthday and introducing her to this living birthday present. She was shaking with shock and excitement the first time she sat on his back and rode slowly round the field talking to him. He was thirteen years old too and what they called a master pony who could teach his rider because he knew what to do. So she learnt to ride that way. He wasn't without his problems because he was very good at jumping, and if he thought the grass looked greener on the other side of the fence, he would hop over it from a standing start. Summers after that included a week at pony club camp and the occasional gymkhana but mostly it was the everyday routine of looking after him that she seemed to enjoy most. John Boy had moved on to a new owner when she left home to go to college but as soon as she had somewhere to live, buying a horse was more important than furniture or food. Her dream now was to own a brood mare and raise very special foals to sell for eventing.

By the time we joined the crowd of walking vegetation back to the bus home we had agreed to start a business together. We would look for some land and she would have somewhere to rear her horses.

It was quite a long time before snails directed their enquiring antennae into the picture.

2a A brief history of snail farming

In the beginning the relationship between woman and snail was quite simple. She was gathering food and snails were there to eat, leaving huge heaps of empty shells in middens all around the Mediterranean some 17,000 years ago. There was no need to farm them then because they hung from the bushes like ripe fruit waiting to be picked. But the relationship became more complicated as time went by.

In the early job demarcation disputes between hunters and gatherers it was probably the women who got the job of gathering snails along with the vegetables for the stew pot. After all, you don't need to strut about wearing war paint with a spear in your hand or hold an important ceremony just to pick a snail off a bush. When the first gardener planted up her vegetable patch, the local snails probably thought she was doing it for their benefit and the battle between gardener and mollusc began in earnest. Of course the gardener could even up the odds by lying in wait and eating the intruders before they ate her lunch. Or she could turn the scheme to her own advantage by creating gardens just to cultivate snails. So it is thought that snails became one of the earliest domesticated animals; kept, not as pets, but as a common part of the diet. If events had continued in the same vein there would have been no need to scatter your back garden with little blue pellets. But Britain was covered with ice when all this was going on so our ancestors were late starters in the snail eating stakes.

Meeting the Romans was a life changing experience for the Brits. It's hard to believe that in a county surrounded by sea, Kentish folk hadn't worked out that fish were for eating. They thought horses were delicious but were soon persuaded to try snails instead. To seafood lovers that would have been a simple change and they remained on the menu for centuries.

But somewhere along the road the relationship turned sour. Maybe some later invader from Scandinavia or the Low Countries turned up their noses. However it happened, snails fell out of favour, especially here in East Kent, where we are so close to France.

3
Managing the transition

Sarah's quirky little car was tucked into a corner of the car park when I arrived at Aylesford Priory. It was a warm day and the long drive with the windows open gave me time to unwind my shoulders out of computer screen mode. It had been a long morning but I'd managed to get a chapter finished and marked some essays. I pulled into the shade of the avenue of trees and switched off the engine. For a moment I leaned back and enjoyed the peacefulness of the place before emerging into the sun. Only bird song; no traffic sounds or human voices. Then I collected my bag from the boot and looked round. The café in the converted barn was functional but not luxurious; appropriate for resting pilgrims. Sarah put down her mobile phone when she saw me, pushed back her wooden chair on the quarry tiled floor, the sound echoing through the rafters, and came towards me with her arms outspread.

'Hello,' she said. 'It feels like ages since I saw you.' She stepped back and studied my face. 'Is it really only a few months? You look ten years younger.'

'Thank you.' I couldn't stop smiling. 'It feels like a lifetime ago, doesn't it?'

'Several lifetimes.' She glanced towards the menu board. 'They've got home-made soup and it smells lovely.'

'That sounds good. I'm hungry.'

We filled our trays and found a table by the window. Outside, the grey flint walls of the Priory contrasted with the grassy softness of their surroundings. Ducks slept on the banks of the pond after an early morning swim. Weeping willows swept fallen leaves from the surface of the water.

'The freelance life is suiting you then?' Sarah said, breaking open a bread roll and spreading it thickly with butter.

'It certainly is.' I took a mouthful of soup. 'Hmm, this is delicious.' I took some bread and chewed thoughtfully. 'Do you know? I feel I've achieved more in the last six months than in the whole of the last six years.'

'Working at home?'

'It is wonderful not having to struggle down the motorway in the rush hour and get home in the dark. I can start and stop work when I like.'

Sarah paused, her spoon halfway to her mouth. 'The danger, of course, is forgetting to stop work.' She looked at me.

I looked down and ran my hand over the smooth wooden surface of the table top. 'It's more complicated than that.' I took some more soup. 'It's made me redefine work.'

'How do you mean?' Sarah looked puzzled.

'I used to think work was what you got paid for and play was what you did the rest of the time.'

'That sounds like a reasonable proposition.'

'But if work is pleasurable why would you want to stop doing it?'

'Come on, you've got to have down time, haven't you?'

'Well, it all depends on how you see things. Work doesn't come in solid blocks of eight hours the way it used to. I can do an hour's writing, then walk to the post office, then mark some essays, cook lunch and then cut the grass. If I want to make some phone calls in the evenings when it's too dark to go outside… answer my emails and do some research for another chapter … instead of slumping in front of the telly … that's not a problem, is it?' I put down my spoon, folded my arms and sat back.

'Hmm.' Sarah chewed.

'You're not convinced,' I said.

I'm thinking about it,' she said. Then she leaned forward. 'It's about looking after yourself. That's what worries me.'

'I'm fine!'

'Hmm.'

I finished my soup and put down my spoon again. 'I've been doing some voluntary work too.'

'How do you fit that in?'

'It's not every day,' I said defensively. 'It's partly about keeping my hand in. When you are on the outside it's easy to get out of touch with what's happening.'

'So what are you doing?'

'I'm working for the mental health trust reviewing cases of detained patients.'

Sarah picked up her knife and cut her bread roll deliberately into very small pieces. 'That sounds like a big responsibility.'

'It is … but the interesting thing to me is that it feels like work even though I'm not being paid.'

'Just be careful you don't take on too much.'

'The boundaries between work and the rest of life have definitely become blurred.'

Sarah put down the knife. 'I'm sure there must be a flaw in your argument somewhere,' she said. 'I just haven't found it yet.' Then she smiled and pointed at the bread. 'Look what you've made me do.'

I laughed, leaning forward to fish the teabag out of the pot and starting to pour. 'Stop worrying. I'm fine!'

'Let's wait and see.'

I held out the teapot. 'Are you ready for a cup?'

'Yes please.'

I filled her cup and handed it to her. 'I've discovered some of the disadvantages of working from home too,' I said. 'I caught a bus the other day and the driver seemed quite surprised when I offered him money. I wanted to say: "Do I look that old?" But then I looked round at all those fit, healthy people with nothing to do except play golf and thought what a waste of talent it was.'

'Maybe they wouldn't see it like that.'

'Maybe not … but I can't see the point in stopping work as long as I can get it.'

'Self-employment as the antidote to retirement?'

'Perhaps.' I looked down into my cup. 'It shook me, actually. I sat on the bus, watching the countryside rush past, thinking I'd better get moving before it's too late. If I don't hurry up and decide what I want to be when I grow up it'll be too late.'

Sarah leaned forward. 'It sounds to me as though you've already got enough to do.'

'Well … at the moment maybe, but I've got to think ahead. I've nearly finished this writing contract. The cash came from the Department of Health and I don't think they're going to come up with any more … and anyway, I think that was just a sort of stop gap. It's not what I really want to do with my life.'

'Can't you find writing contracts elsewhere? There must be other people commissioning textbooks.'

'There are.' I looked at the ceiling; the pattern of oak beams stretched out like the webbed fingers of a hand. 'The other day someone asked me to write a training pack for NVQ level 2 in Customer Care.'

Sarah wrinkled her nose. 'Oh! What did you say?'

'I said I was really busy… couldn't possibly fit them in this side of next Christmas.'

'…or the one after that.'

'Exactly!'

Sarah sighed. 'So what's your bright idea then?'

'I want to grow food. I think farming is deeply

embedded in the British psyche. For me it's very close to the surface and I think it is for lots of people. Just think about all those people digging away on their allotments. All those chicken coops and community pig rearing schemes feed into this need we have to grow our own food.'

Sarah shook her head. 'I'm quite happy to pop down to the supermarket for my food actually.'

'I met up with Rebecca a few weeks ago. We went to the Chelsea Flower Show and had a lovely day together. But best of all, we had a long conversation about what we wanted to do with the rest of our lives. Rebecca's been looking round for a field and I got an email this morning to tell me she's found something she wants me to go and look at. The auction's in a few weeks' time. If we're going to grow stuff we need somewhere to do it.'

We drove down a narrow farm track between high hedges, catching glimpses of arable crops to one side and cows to the other. A cloud of bright little birds took to the air noisily as we walked along beside the water-filled ditch to the pond. The Coventry Canal was nearby, but it was quite a distance from the nearest house. A wide gateway opened into a boot-shaped meadow and we stood and gazed at the glorious view before stepping over the threshold to walk the boundary. A drainage ditch ran under the hedge on each side, widening to form a pond under a clump of mature ash trees. It had been ploughed and planted with grass but there were still wild flowers underfoot. The horses would need some cover but it was just what we were looking for.

The auction at Uttoxeter Racecourse had been a tense affair but we held our nerve and outbid our rivals. The field was ours. Within months Rebecca had bought her first brood mare, carefully selected a suitable sire and the first foal was on the way.

But there was a problem. Horses tend to cost money rather than make it. We needed to find an agricultural activity that Rebecca could manage alongside the horses that would bring in a reasonable income. So the search was on.

3a Old English recipe 'to dress snayles'

I was interested to find recipes for snails dating back centuries showing that snails were familiar items on the English menu. This recipe from seventeenth century England looks surprisingly familiar in flavours as the snails are served with garlic, onions and fresh herbs. But there's no butter included. The author says that this soup is very nourishing, and was reputed to be a treatment for consumption. I've translated the Old English to make it easier to understand.

(Note: I've seen quite a few recipes where the snails are killed slowly by heating them up gradually. It's not a method I would recommend as I'm not convinced it is humane.)

To dresse snayles. (The Compleat Cook, Nathaniel Brook, 1658)

Take your Snayles and wash them very well in many waters. After that put them in a White Earthen Pan, or very wide Dish, and put as much water as will cover them, then heat them up slowly. The Snayles will come out of the shells and die. Take them out of the pan and wash them very well in salted water. Then boil them in a pan with more clean salted water for about twenty minutes, to take away the slime. Pour them through a colander to drain.

Heat some good quality oil, slice two or three onions in it, and let them fry well. Then put the

Snayles into the oil with the onions, and let them stew together a little. After that put them all into an earthenware pan and cover with water and bring them to the boil. Season them with salt, and let them simmer gently for three or four hours.

Chop parsley, pennyroyal, fennel, thyme, and put them in a mortar to crush them as for a green sauce. Add some breadcrumbs soaked in the soup or pottage from the Snayles, and dissolve it all in the mortar with a little saffron and cloves well beaten to make a thickening for the soup. Let the herbs stew in the soup, and when you serve it up, squeeze a little fresh lemon juice and vinegar. If you put a clove of garlic in the mortar with the herbs, it will improve the flavour. Serve the soup in a dish with croutons.

(re-published with thanks to Janet at The Old Foodie www.theoldfoodie.com)

4
Doing what the
Romans did

Kent is synonymous with the production of food. Growing, hunting and fishing are all around us. I can eat well all year round on local food. So we started to look round for a food business that Rebecca and I could manage between us. We looked at all sorts of ideas. I got a book from the library on inland carp farming but the set up costs would have been high and I wasn't sure there was a market. Rabbits were a possibility, either for food or angora. For a while I was quite taken with the idea of farming rabbits for fibre. We toyed with the idea of raising guinea fowl or quail but they can be very noisy. Then one day I was trawling the internet and found a site on farm diversification. Amongst the suggestions was one that leapt off the screen at me: snail farming. Once the idea had come it wouldn't leave me alone. I was waking up at night thinking about it and wondering if this was what we had been looking for.

The influence of the Roman invasion is inescapable in this part of England, from the remains of the enormous gateway at Richborough to the well-preserved mosaic floors of their villas. Every day we drive on their long straight roads. An even greater influence is the way they changed our diet. Most of the fruit, vegetables and herbs we rely on were first grown here by the Romans. One of the delicacies they introduced to our tables was snails. I read that the rare Roman snails could still be found on sites associated with Roman occupation, so I went searching for them.

Near where I live is a sunken lane which, in the past, was the way people walked to and from the well. The high banks are held together with tree roots and beneath the canopy of leaves daylight disappears. It's a place where I could imagine highwaymen hiding in the branches, lying in wait for their victims. Here on the map the contour lines crowd close together where ice and water have cut through the limestone escarpment, creating deep valleys. The river, reduced now to a modest flow, used to be wide enough for Roman galleys.

To reach the wood, I drove along a lane so narrow that no one could pass. Old man's beard and wild hops festooned the hedgerows and fanned me through the open windows. In the middle of the road, tufts of grass broke through the tarmac skin. I tucked my car into the wide corner of a junction out of the way of marauding tractors and set off on foot down the bridle path between the trees. The early afternoon sun filtered through the branches of mature beech, oak and hazel coppice. Miniature forests of moss and lichen and ripples of bracket fungi covered piles of cut branches left lying on the ground. Smells of damp decay and fox hung in the air. The mud, softened by the previous night's rain, was marked with fresh hoof prints from an early morning rider. After the first stumble I watched out for protruding flints. The woodland floor was uneven with ridges of chalk and flints running parallel with the contours, some of them topped with willows. They were pollarded when young so they looked like a child's drawing of a tree, with a bunch of branches bursting out of the trunk. These lines denoted old boundaries between the properties of different families.

The path began to slope downwards past ancient yew and butcher's broom. As I walked on down the hill, rabbits started up from behind every rotting tree stump and I heard the sound of a pheasant calling in the distance. A single shot rang out and I missed my footing with surprise, the briars catching at my sleeve. Where the path forked I stopped to check the map and noticed the silence. It couldn't be much further. At the bottom of the valley the woodland ended abruptly and the path opened out.

The meadow vegetation was well-grazed but dotted with flowers and probably undisturbed for centuries. The soil was thin over the chalk and a plough would not have made much impression. Standing there, it was easy to imagine how the landscape used to be. There were no human signs, no pylons marching across the hill and no buildings. I wondered if there was once a Roman villa. This is where I found them, just as I'd been told, on the warm edge of the wood, the shells heavy and chalky white among the leaf litter.

Roman snails don't travel fast or far, even in a lifetime. Even after 2000 years, colonies of snails remain in secret places as evidence of Roman occupation. They live on undisturbed limestone grassland, well drained slopes of river valleys, old railway embankments, open rides through native woodland, along boundaries, hedgerows or roadside banks protected from the prevailing wind. They're protected now as growth and replacement is too slow to support collection for the pot.

I crouched for a while, turning an empty shell in my hand and thinking. The last textbook was ready to be ring bound and my OU students were sitting their exam. It was time to do something about this fledgling business idea. In spare moments I'd been trying to find out more about farming snails but I couldn't seem to find out what I wanted to know. I was sure that if I looked in the right place there had to be something on the web. I'd spent several days talking to agricultural colleges but they didn't know anything about it and told me I'd have to go to France to learn more.

I stood up and re-traced my steps back home. Taking a deep breath, I plugged myself into the world wide web and resumed trawling.

4a Farming and cooking snails the Roman way

In Roman times snails were considered a delicacy. It is thought that the Romans were the first people to farm snails rather than just collecting them from the wild. The snails were kept on land surrounded by water to prevent them from escaping. They were fed on milk, wine must and spelt wheat. Wine must is the freshly crushed grapes, the juice, seeds, skins and stems before they are fermented. For the final fattening they were kept in jars with air holes with a milk and salt mixture. Slaves would regularly clean away the snail excrement. When they became too fat to get back in their shells they were fried in oil and served with liquamen (a salty fermented fish sauce) mixed with wine. This modern day version is as true to the original in preparation as possible but is not recommended as a humane method.

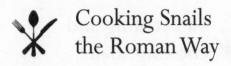

Cooking Snails the Roman Way

Ingredients

Assuming 6 edible snails per person, for every 6 snails you need:

2 pints of milk

plenty of salt

1 teaspoon of Thai fish sauce

1 tablespoon of wine vinegar

Method

Clean the snails.

Put the snails in a bucket with half the milk and salt for one day.

Transfer to a fresh vessel containing the remaining milk for one more day, cleaning away the excrement every hour.

When the snails are fattened, so they can no longer return to their shells, fry them slowly in oil until they are tender.

Serve cold with a dressing made from Thai fish sauce and wine.

5
The search is on

The search for information was long and hard. I knew the theoretical basics about molluscs from my science education but we wanted to know how to set up a commercial enterprise. There were a few academic research papers and some old stuff dating back a few decades when it seemed lots of people in Britain had tried to farm snails. I was curious about that boom and why it had died. But there was nothing specific, till I came across a name. Scrolling down the web pages I spotted a reference to a snail centre in East Anglia.

'I've found something that looks like a possible lead.' I managed to catch Rebecca on the phone. 'If I can get hold of this guy and fix up a visit will you be able to get time off to come?'

I rang the number and waited. It was a long shot and I wondered if he would still be in business. If he was, would he be willing to share his knowledge?

'How did you find me?' Michael's voice was friendly and encouraging. 'I used to run courses in the old days but I haven't done that for ages.'

It turned out Michael was still farming snails and he was quite happy for us to visit and see what he was doing, so we decided to go. A misty morning found us driving along country lanes through the East Anglian countryside. His cottage was next to the silent, empty sheds of a cattle farm that had just been auctioned off. To reach the door Rebecca and I walked through the garden between raised vegetable beds of beautiful black fenland soil. When our knock was answered, Michael's wife pointed to the row of semi-cylindrical Nissen huts, like metal polytunnels, squatting along the fence line.

'You'll find him in one of those,' she said. 'If you go down I'll give him a ring and let him know you're here.' With that she disappeared inside and closed the door firmly against the wind blowing keenly from the east across the flat fields that stretched to the horizon.

Michael emerged squinting into the daylight, his weather-beaten face smiling warmly, mobile phone to his ear. 'Good morning,' he called out, and held out his hand. 'You found us then? Come on in, come on. It's too cold to stand out here.' We followed him into a warm anteroom where a boiler purred and he closed the door behind us, shutting out the light. Then he pushed through a row of heavy plastic strips into the softly padded interior. Although it was a bleak day outside, here it was as warm and humid as the jungle. The smell was of warm damp earth, like the woody fragrance of mushrooms on a forest floor after autumn rain. In the low lighting, all I could see at first were rows of plastic boxes.

Michael was kind and helpful, listening to our questions and explaining that he was farming African snails and they needed to be kept in the sort of conditions they would experience at home. Unprotected, they wouldn't cope with the English climate at all. He gave us a booklet he'd produced for would-be snail farmers during the eighties and talked about his experience of selling from market stalls. I asked him about the boom and why the bubble had burst.

'Eating snails just seemed to go out of fashion for a while,' he said. 'But there's still enough people wanting them to make it worthwhile.' Then he opened a box and lifted out a snail for us to see. Its elegant shell was black and conical, like the water snails I'd kept as a child.

'These aren't your ordinary French escargots, of course,' he said. 'But I harvest them small and sell them in garlic butter just the same.'

I held a warm snail in my hand until it came out to see what was going on. Lifting it closer to my face, I could see its eyes on the end of its long antennae. 'Hello,' I said. 'It's good to meet you.' The snail stretched out its glossy grey body and looked in my direction enquiringly. I really felt this was something I could do.

Rebecca and I sat outside in the car afterwards, talking for a long time about what we'd learnt. I was sure that I wanted to farm snails – but were African snails the right kind? We thought about the cost and environmental impact of keeping them warm and wondered how big the market was for African snails in Britain. That was a bit of an unknown. Maybe we should think again.

I went back to my internet search through page after page of nothing useful. Weeks later, suddenly, there on a tourist board website I found another lead. The tourist office gave me the details but said they weren't sure whether he was still open for business. Peter advertised courses and visits and for day after day I kept on ringing but only got the answer phone. I left messages but he didn't return my calls. There was no email address so in desperation I wrote him a letter and waited...and waited. But he didn't respond. The fruitless weeks were turning into months and it was nearly Christmas before I wondered whether to give up. Should I get in the car and just drive there and hope he would let me in? But it was a long way and he might be out of the country for all I knew.

I needed to give it one more go. I picked up the phone and dialled the number. I knew it off by heart, I'd rung it so many times. I held my breath.

'Hello?'

I was so surprised when he answered that I almost forgot what I wanted to say. I'd struck lucky and caught him. Now here I was, stumbling over my words. 'Hello,'

I said. 'At last!'

Peter was encouraging about the proposed venture, promising that if we got started he would buy our produce at 4p a snail and save us the bother of marketing. Even before I worked out the costs 4p each didn't sound very much, but I didn't like to say. He told me he had been running his operation for twenty years and was selling to all the famous Michelin star restaurants. When I asked about the practicalities of setting up he spoke at length in general terms but was very vague about the details. I asked if we could visit but there was no way he was going to let us see his operation. My optimism flagged when he said he was no longer running courses and wasn't open to the public any more. By the time I put down the phone I just wanted to cry.

So I gave up on him and carried on trawling the net. If I'd found one lead maybe there was another out there. Then one day I suppose I must have put different key words into the search engine, though I can't remember now, but there it was: a site advertising snails for sale and offering a day's consultancy for would-be farmers.

A few weeks later I found myself travelling to Devon on the train. Rebecca had not been able to get the time off work at short notice to come with me, so I was tasked with collecting all the information I could and reporting back. The farm was in a hamlet at the bottom of a valley; a handful of cottages were scattered on the hillsides above the single track line. Beside the station platform stood the red brick remains of an ancient Royal Mail sorting office, now redundant. Following the map, I walked up the lane between dry stone walls towards the only tall building in sight; an imposing red brick façade declared its dominance over the landscape. I could see a Dutch barn behind and a clutch of low tiled buildings huddled in the cobbled yard to the side. The first obstacle was attached to the warm wet nose thrusting at me through the bars of the gate. Rex wasn't pleased to see me but his owner was more welcoming. For a whole morning I sat in Frank's grubby farmhouse watching a large cockroach crawl up the wall behind his head while he talked and chain smoked. From time to time a small child would put its head round the door to stare. There were four young children in the house and we were occupying their play space. The kitchen, where the snails were supposedly cooked and prepared for market, was festooned with wet washing.

The day was punctuated by the arrival of Cornish pasties hot from the oven, served with a big mug of tea.

'I haven't actually got any snails at the moment as we're selling up and planning to emigrate,' Frank said. 'My wife wants to be near her dad now he's getting old.' He grinned and took a large bite of pasty.

I stopped chewing and looked out of the window. If he hadn't got any snails to show me what was I doing here?

He swallowed and carried on: 'But you can see the set up and all my equipment is for sale, which would cut the cost of your initial investment.'

That made sense, I suppose. I carried on eating.

After lunch we went outside, leaving Rex the dog leaping up and down with rage behind the shed door. Inside the barn, concealed from view, was a big insulated polytunnel. Frank opened the door and we walked into a warm damp atmosphere, walls green with algae and moss, like the entrance to a cave. Spiders had taken up residence, and fine cobwebs caught in my hair and clothes. I had to use my imagination as Frank walked up and down the lines of shelving and empty boxes demonstrating how he looked after the snails. Before I left he gave me a copy of his own version of 'Snail Rearing for Dummies'. He talked extensively about the market and assured me there was room for another 50 farms the same size as his.

As I sat on the train going home, reading the book, picturing myself in his shoes (without the cockroach, of course), I wondered where I was going to get my breeding stock from if he didn't have any. My search wasn't over yet.

I persisted, and after more long telephone calls, I managed to persuade Peter to sell me some breeders.

5a Farming and cooking African snails

African land snails are commonly kept as pets in Britain but they are edible too, and in West Africa – particularly Ghana and Nigeria – they are a common part of the diet. When African peoples migrate they want to carry on eating the kinds of food they had at home so there is a market for African snails in Britain. I've heard that you can buy them live from stalls in some of the London streets. These would normally be imported, of course, and there have been some anxieties about health and safety if they have been collected from the wild.

From a farming point of view, the advantages of African over European snails is that they live longer – up to 10 years, get much bigger and lay a lot more eggs. The main disadvantage is that to successfully rear them you need to mimic tropical jungle conditions.

African Soup

I've looked at Nigerian recipes that include snails and this one is based on afang soup. Afang is the name of a leaf vegetable but as we are going to substitute spinach perhaps it should be called spinach soup. Many of the African recipes that I've seen are substantial one pot stews combining meat and fish with vegetables.

Ingredients

500g cubed red meat (shin beef, venison, offal)

enough snails so that each person will get a few

500g white fish, skin and bones removed

500g washed spinach

oil to fry

500ml vegetable or fish stock

1 hot chilli pepper left whole for a milder heat or chopped if spicy is preferred

1 large onion

1 cup shrimps or prawns

Method

I think a slow cooker would be a good choice of container for this recipe.

In a large pot heat a few cups of stock to a near boil

and add the meat. Cook for a few minutes on high heat then add the onion and chilli pepper. Reduce the heat, cover and simmer.

In a separate pan bring a few cups of salted water to a boil. Drop the washed snails into the boiling water and cook for two or three minutes. Remove snails from water, cool them under running water so you can handle them and use a small fork to remove the snails from their shells. Wash the snail meat and rinse with lime or lemon juice. Add the snails to the pot with the meat. Cover and simmer for an hour at least.

Add the spinach, the fish and the shrimp or prawns to the pot. Add more water, broth, or stock as needed and bring back to the boil. Adjust the seasoning. Cover and continue to simmer until everything is completely cooked and tender.

Serve with bread or rice or potatoes.

6
Virgin farmers

It was still dark when the alarm went off but I was already awake, worried about oversleeping. Today was the big day – I was actually getting some snails! Peter had eventually agreed to sell me some breeders and all I had to do now was meet him at dawn in a quiet back street away from the public gaze. East Kent commuters have to start early and there was quite a queue of us fretting behind the milk tanker by the time we hit the by-pass. The first load of lorries had already disembarked from Dover and pulled into the layby at the breakfast van to leave the road for those of us in a hurry. Then it was straight up the A2 and turn left into a traffic jam. I wasn't used to driving in London, or watching out for taxis cutting in close from the right, cyclists squeezing along the bike lane to my left, cars dodging into the bus lane and motorbikes weaving in and out, knitting the whole jangling chaos together. At each junction arrows pointed in all directions. The place names were familiar but I had only a faintly drawn map in my head to follow.

I was late. The city streets and sky were painted grey but for the double yellow lines shrieking beneath my wheels. I perched there, wondering what time traffic wardens started work. The tension of the journey was knotted into my neck so I took the risk, turned off the engine and crawled out. I'd arranged to meet Peter an hour ago round the back of a pub near Blackfriars Bridge but the curtains were closed. I could see no lights through the glass door and there was no response to my tentative knock. I pulled up the zip on my fleece against the November air. I could feel the moisture settling on my face and hair like a cobweb. It was a snail friendly morning.

By the time he arrived I was resigning myself to having missed him. But there he was at last, and in the back of his car was a box.

'So you know all about snail farming, do you?' he asked as he handed it to me.

I smiled and thanked him as I took the box, feeling its weight on my aching arms. The snails were much heavier than I expected and I could hear a faint rustling noise as I put it carefully into the boot of the car. 'Have you got time for coffee?' I asked.

He looked at his watch. 'Okay,' he said. 'I'm running late but I expect Carlo will have the coffee on.'

The right kind of knock on the door produced a response. Bolts were drawn, keys turned and it was opened cautiously. An overpowering smell of stale beer and cigarettes hit me in the face. I took a deep breath before diving into the dark interior. Peter spoke in low tones to the barman and made his way to a corner table. A few moments later two cups of pale milky coffee were thrown down before us and Peter gulped his in one go. I opened my mouth to ask a question but he pre-empted me by sliding an invoice across the table towards me. I gave him the cash. He counted it quickly, then slipped it into an inside pocket and stood up.

'Sorry I haven't got time to chat,' he said, and he moved towards the door.

I gulped down my coffee and followed. He still wasn't going to tell me anything helpful.

When I got back to the car I opened the box and looked down at my investment. In groups of 50, my breeding stock were unceremoniously sealed in plastic perforated bread wrapping and stacked with corrugated card between each layer. It took me two hours to get home again and I worried about them getting too cold. When I took each bag out of the box they were lying side by side, upside down, tucked up in their shells, unmoving – and I wondered if they would last the night.

This was the start of something new. Their room was ready and it was a bit like bringing a baby home from hospital. The first time I left them in the house on their own I worried whether they would be alright. The weight of responsibility suddenly felt enormous. These three hundred little bodies were entirely dependent on me to keep them alive. I wasn't confident and there was no midwife to advise me.

In any relationship, you have to live together to really get to know each other. That's when you discover that your beloved has all those irritating little habits: they snore, pick their nose, or invite all their mates round to shout at the referee when the football's on TV. Snails are nocturnal and every night it sounded like they were having a party. It was like living near a busy nightclub or railway line: after a while you get used to the sound of the 4.45 to Euston vibrating through your bedroom, or late night revellers being sick in your front garden. So I got used to the way the snails crashed about at night, climbing up onto the lid of their boxes and falling during their nocturnal goings on. I don't know if it's fun or just a quicker way of getting down.

My clothes took second place in the airing cupboard to trays of incubating snail eggs, which needed to be kept warm. Each day I looked to see if anything had changed and found myself filled with pleasure as the white eggs slowly turned into a heap of minute golden snails. At first they behaved like a flock of sheep on a hillside, flowing across the compost and up the sides of the lid. When I sprayed them with water they separated and spread out across the surface, scooping up the water, waving their impossibly long antennae. Gradually, over the months, they turned from little opals into animated humbugs.

It was time to share the care so I gave Rebecca a call.

Motorway service stations make convenient meeting places, however dreadful they are. In these plastic transit palaces everyone seems to have that glazed look that comes from travelling long distances on boring roads. On weekdays businessmen may stop and hold a meeting, laptop on table, mobile in hand. Holidaymakers, fearful of falling asleep at the wheel, stop for a comfort break from time to time, downing a quick cup of caffeine and a sugary snack before rejoining the slow trek north or southwards. These arteries, which were supposed to speed up journeys, so often slow to a crawl. On Sundays there are families looking tired and confused, children crying and slot machines ringing. The food is designed to be grabbed and swallowed in a hurry. Clothing and toy concessions, a food boutique and sometimes a bookshop give an air of the big railway station or airport departure lounge.

In the car park, on the day we met, two policemen sat in their car watching the groups of young men who lounged and swaggered around their customised cars. Hair was groomed in rear view mirrors, collars turned up to frame chiselled features and jeans hung low on narrow hips. There was definitely a tension in the air, like the Jets and Sharks in West Side Story.

The service station, just three miles away from where I used to live, had smothered land that I must have walked across as a child, when motorways were just a gleam in Mr Marples' eye. It was strange to come back here and see familiar names on the signposts pointing to places that were no longer the same. Once I went back to the village where I'd lived and saw with adult eyes how much bigger the houses looked and how much smarter they had become. I was seven when we'd moved there from London, and the village had just started expanding. It had seemed like the country to me, with open spaces full of ponds to fish and trees to climb. It was the fields of ragwort covered in striped cinnabar moth caterpillars that I remembered so clearly, and our tin bath full of newts. All of it had disappeared beneath a four lane motorway and this monstrous carbuncle called South Mimms Services.

When Rebecca and I started to empty the car of boxes of snails I was conscious, out of the corner of my eye, of the two policemen watching us, but they must have decided we were just a couple of harmless cranks. Nobody else took any notice at all. It was good to meet and this was halfway, however uninviting the premises. There was lots to talk about but all too soon we were back on the road. It was the first of many meetings to swap snails and discuss the latest developments.

That first year the snails surprised me by mating at what seemed a precocious age, elbowing each other out of the way in their drive to lay eggs. Each morning the laying boxes looked like the battle of the Somme, with trenches, dugouts and craters everywhere and every snail covered in mud. Soon I had more eggs than I knew what to do with. Every tray I could lay hands on was full of glistening heaps. The snail room was bursting at the seams.

When people heard the snails lived in the spare bedroom, they always asked if they could escape. Perhaps they imagined me waking up in the night and finding a small moist body snuggled up on the pillow, or silver trails over the fridge door after a midnight feast. The answer was that they could get out of their housing: if they all lined up and pushed against the cover, it sometimes gave way. But they didn't go far; they just mooched about for a bit, then sat on the top of the box waiting to be let back in. If I could invent a snail version of the cat flap, they'd probably have returned by themselves. After all, everything they wanted was in the box. The air was too dry outside and their food and water and all their mates were inside.

Still, the snail room door was shut at night, just in case.

6a Farming and cooking snails in Italy

Snail farming is a big industry in modern Italy, particularly in the north centred around Cherasco where there is a snail breeding centre: Istituto Internazionale di Elicicoltura di Cherasco. There is a college for training farmers. They sell equipment and supplies, including breeding stock and market snails for local producers. The picture on the cover of their snail breeding manual shows a snail farm on a hillside that looks just like a vineyard from a distance.

Snails are widely eaten in Italy, incorporated into many meals that sound familiar – such as in a tomato based sauce with rice or pasta. The title of this recipe seems to hark back to history but the flavours are very different from the Roman way of cooking snails.

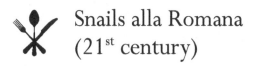

Snails alla Romana (21ˢᵗ century)

Ingredients

For one and a half kilos of snails:

1 litre tomato sauce - your favourite recipe from fresh tomatoes or tinned

a cayenne pepper, roughly chopped

a handful of fresh basil

2 glasses of white wine

2 cloves of garlic, crushed

1 tablespoonful of oil to fry

salt and pepper to taste

grated parmesan cheese to garnish

Method

Boil the snails for 30 minutes and then shell them. In a saucepan put the crushed cloves of garlic and chopped cayenne pepper with a spoonful of oil and brown them gently. Add the tomato sauce, cook for 20 minutes with the white wine, add salt and pepper with the basil. Finally add the snails and cook for at least an hour until they are soft. Serve with pasta, with parmesan cheese grated over the top.

Ravioli stuffed with snails

Ingredients

For 4 dozen cooked snails you will need:

Pasta dough made with 200g flour

100gms mixed mushrooms

200g ricotta cheese

Clove of garlic

25g shallots

a glass of white wine

chopped chives to garnish

oil to fry the mushrooms

butter to fry the ravioli

Method

Mince or chop the cooked snails and prepare the filling for the ravioli by combining them with the ricotta cheese and herbs. Roll out the pasta dough, cut into squares and sandwich the squares together with the filling, sealing the edges carefully. Make a sauce with shallots, sliced mushrooms, parsley and garlic. Boil the ravioli in salted water, drain and brown in a pan with butter. Serve the ravioli in a hot dish with the mushroom sauce and garnished with chopped chives.

(Many thanks to Istituto Elicicocultura for recipe ideas)

7

Construction

If you've got a few spare kilos to lose then I can recommend a way of losing them. I like to think I'm quite good at making things but putting up the poly-tunnel nearly killed me. With just a couple of hours' work a day my waist whittled down to wasp-like proportions.

Back in the 1980s, the last time there was a boom in snail farming, one of the ways people kept them was to let them loose in a poly-tunnel. The hurricane of '87, however, put a stop to many a young enterprise. Okay, so it wasn't a real hurricane, but here in Kent it certainly felt like one. Plastic doesn't stand up well in a gale and the occupants no doubt galloped off over the hill and spread themselves far and wide before dawn broke. In early summer a decade later the sun was shining, and all that history was forgotten. A poly-tunnel seemed like the best way to make more space for my burgeoning population of snail babies.

The website said: '*Creating your own micro-climate has never been easier. With a polytunnel every ray of sunshine works a little harder, every drop of rain is managed, damaging winds are kept at bay...and frost damage is a thing of the past.*' It sounded ideal. The website assured its readers that most domestic sized installations could be done within a day and the instructions were fantastically easy to understand. If I got stuck their construction expert Doug was there on the end of the telephone waiting for my call. He smiled at me from the screen and I felt sure we would get on well. 'Get ready; get set; go!' said the promotional video. So I did.

I paced about the garden for some time before settling on the right location, attracting the attention of next door's cat. It stalked two paces behind me, tail aloft, waiting for me to do something interesting. I didn't want to displace any trees and I needed to be able to walk all round it. Behind the shed, it would be close enough to the house for power and water but hidden from view. Measuring with a sharp metal retractable tape is an art, especially if it is spring loaded. I trapped my fingers several times before discovering that a brick on the end is quite an effective way of stopping it from curling up when you let go. But it introduces the unfortunate possibility of inaccuracy, even if the tape doesn't become a catapult. Anyway, I measured the space as best I could and ordered the tunnel online. It came by lorry next day and the driver was not best pleased to have to unload it. He was a big man: over six foot and muscular, but he struggled with the bags of metal poles and big roll of plastic. It took him a while to drag them out of the back of the lorry and drop them over the tailgate onto the ground with a clang and a thump. Then he jumped down and dragged them off the road, protecting his back carefully as he did so. He stood there for a moment, breathing heavily, and with hands on hips looked down on me. 'Best of luck,' he said, and made his getaway. Alarm bells started to ring. My first task would be to get the bags from the front garden round to the back. I grabbed hold of the end of one of the bags and pulled nonchalantly, in case anyone was watching. It didn't move. So I retired from the scene in a dignified way to put the kettle on, and I sat down to think the problem through. The solution was obvious, of course: all I had to do was unpack the bits so I could lift them a few at a time. Intelligence could make any task achievable. It took me the best part of the day and most of my daily quota of expendable energy to shift the bits from the front to the back of the house.

On the first day of construction I stood looking at the chosen space with the DIY guide that made it all sound so easy in my hand. 'Dig six holes half a metre wide and half a metre deep.' Digging holes was never my strong point. I had a nice stainless steel spade. It was quite small and dainty; I think they used to call it a lady's spade, probably designed for a little light work on the herbaceous border. If the soil condition was just right I could usually get it into the ground by putting all my weight onto the blade, perhaps even stamping on it. I then leaned back, arms extended, to pull against the handle and lever the blade upwards. When the blade came up, of course, I often found myself sitting on the ground. As long as the blade hadn't collected too much soil I could then usually lift and empty it to one side. So I got my spade out of the shed and enthusiastically threw the blade at the ground. Although it was still early summer the weather had been hot and dry for weeks, as it often is in June. The soil was clay, with flints over chalk, and the clay had set hard as a rock. Throwing the spade down at it just left my elbow, shoulder, indeed the right hand side of my whole body ringing with the impact. Without rain, it would be impossible to dig even if it wasn't for the flints. I decided it was time to introduce myself to Doug on the helpline.

The phone was answered by a deep rich voice that I can only describe as fruity, with a hint of 'Last of the Summer Wine' about it. It was reassuring: this was a man with experience who would know what to do. I hate asking for help; I like to see myself as self-sufficient and able to cope in any crisis, so we didn't get to the point straight away, but he was a very good listener.

The solution was obvious: either get a man in to dig the holes for me, or water the ground to soften it up. "Getting a man in" was way down my list of desirable solutions. I wanted to do this myself. So the pond slowly went down over the following few days, leaving the occupants stranded, as I attempted to soften the ground just enough to get through it. A large pile of nobbly flints accumulated along the fence line but it wasn't hard to find a home for the small amount of actual soil removed. To be honest the holes weren't as big as they suggested but I reckoned they would have to do.

Drilling holes in ancient concrete was another task I hadn't tried before. These instructions were certainly full of surprises. When I was exhausting myself toiling away in the hot sun over the latest simple easy to follow instruction, I wondered many times if I would have ordered the thing at all had I been able to read them beforehand. After bouncing the hammer drill around on the concrete like a pogo stick for a while, I decided to talk to my friend Doug again. He recognised my trembling voice straight away, which was gratifying. 'Hello,' he said, 'I thought it was you.' I told him the whole story and he listened sympathetically. I think he must have trained with the Samaritans. But he couldn't make up for my lack of brawn.

With the big holes dug, I had to wield my wooden mallet to bang in pegs, then balance planks across them with the spirit level wobbling precariously on top. I walked round from corner to corner with my pegs, planks and spirit level, trying to get the base level and square. But somehow they seemed to shift as soon as I let go. I went round and round getting more and more exasperated until I gave up and decided that, like the holes, the corners would just have to do.

The curved hoops looked like the easy bit: rather like a giant version of a child's toy. Lying on the ground, the poles slotted together in a very satisfying way, but then I had to get them upright and of course they were heavy. It was really a two person job to slot them into the waiting holes in the ground but there was only me. So I put the kettle on and had another think. I sat in the shade for a few restful moments, mug of tea in my hand, looking at the hoops lying on the ground. Next door's cat had wisely moved out of harm's way up onto the shed roof where he sat smiling down on me, obviously enjoying the cabaret. There was a question on his face: 'How are you going to get out of that one then?' I put down my empty mug and put the plan into action. I just had to deal with one end at a time. So one end of the hoop went over a hole on one side and I lifted the other end to put it into the opposite hole. Well, it wasn't quite as easy as that but after a lot of false starts the tunnel actually began to look like a tunnel and I began to breathe more easily.

For a few moments I thought I'd cracked it. But when I looked up to admire my handiwork I realised the hoops were way above my head and I had to find a way of getting the ridge pole in place and the plastic cover onto them. I'd seen lots of workmen on building sites shooting up a long ladder carrying what they needed across their shoulders. So I put up the stepladder in the middle of the hoops and slowly climbed up until I was wobbling on the top with the ridge pole pressing down on one shoulder. My hands were full of clips so I couldn't hold on and it felt very precarious but I managed to fix it up and retired exhausted.

The plastic sheet wasn't called heavy duty for nothing. Just moving it about was no mean feat for a five foot two inch eight stone weakling. It came folded so I had to begin by unfolding it. My garden is long and thin with lots of obstacles in it, like trees and flowerbeds and ponds, so it wasn't easy to find the space to spread out this enormous sheet of plastic. I decided to roll it up, thinking if I could get the roll over the end hoop it shouldn't be too difficult to unroll it back over the rest. With great difficulty, and with some of the weight taken by the ladder, I managed to lift one end of the roll of plastic over the ridge pole. Then all I had to do was unroll it to the other end. There was a bit more to it than that, of course.

Making the door was quite satisfying. The pieces were all cut to size. All I had to do was spread them out on the ground and fit them together. On the ground the door and frame fitted perfectly, one inside the other, but when they were hung, of course, they both distorted just enough to leave frustrating gaps. But by then I was too tired to care. Every job had taken three or four times as long as I thought it should. A simple instruction to fix one thing to another gave me hours of frustration as there was always a knot in the wood just where I wanted to cut or drill. Or two pieces which should have lined up just didn't. Just to finish me off, the bottom edges of the plastic cover had to be nailed down to wooden bars around the base. There was a limit to how long I could work in the hot sun with my head hanging down, swinging a hammer and occasionally hitting a nail. But I persevered and eventually the day came when I could step back and admire my handiwork. The silver coated insulation made it look like it had landed from Mars.

By the end of the summer the garden had re-established control. It was more or less hidden from public view by honeysuckle, pink clematis montana, and runner beans climbing the bronze fennel. I felt I couldn't just let the snails loose in there as they might work out how to open the door. So I made some makeshift pens with wire frames and fabric covers. If I'm stuck with a problem, sewing always seem to feature in the solution. They seemed to like their new homes and quite literally expanded to fit the extra space – apparently growing a few millimetres overnight. But they couldn't resist the desire to go exploring – perhaps they were homesick for their nice warm trays indoors. For whatever reason, each day I found intrepid wanderers on the walls and ceiling. Other livestock took up residence too. When I opened the door I was conscious of rapid movement as lots of little legs carried intruders out of sight. Pale woodlice shared this space, rolling up into a ball when I touched them. Spiders hung about waiting for something edible to pass by and I often emerged with strands of silk tangled in my hair. The frogs and toads posed more of a threat to an adventurous young snail. I'd known the frogs and toads since they were tadpoles in the pond and watched them grow, but I didn't feel under any obligation to provide them with a ready source of food. They sat in the corners while I fed the snails; wedge shaped green heads, big eyes and pulsing throats. A tiny toadlet caught me by surprise too, lurking brown in the compost and jumping when I touched him. I was constantly removing slugs from the food bowls but the worms were welcome visitors as they cleaned up the soil and kept it sweet.

It was a good summer and soon I had snails to sell.

7a Cooking snails in Spain

The time for snail festivals in Spain is in spring, when they first emerge from hibernation after the winter.

Snails are a traditional ingredient of paella in Valencia, especially tiny pale mountain snails which are combined with runner beans and butter beans. The Spanish also eat freshwater snails. They roast the snails on a metal sheet with lots of herbs and eat them with bread and aioli (garlic mayonnaise) and wine.

In certain parts of Spain small snails are sold, accompanied by a spicy sauce, by street vendors.

 # Spicy Sauce

Ingredients

large onion, chopped

olive oil to fry

two cloves garlic, chopped

one leek, chopped

a green pepper, seeded and chopped

half kilo ripe tomatoes, chopped

2 dried whole chillies – remove before blending

a bay leaf

lots of fresh black pepper

squeeze of lemon juice

good handful of chopped parsley

Method

Cook a kilo of small snails in boiling salted water for 30 minutes then put them into the blended sauce to cook for a further 30 minutes. Part of the pleasure comes from picking them out of the shells – like you would winkles.

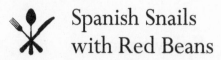

Spanish Snails with Red Beans

Snails are a common ingredient in the Barcelona region of Spain. This recipe has the aniseed flavour of Pernod combined with the heat of red chillies.

Ingredients

4 tbsp olive oil

2 tbsp unsalted butter

50g shallots, finely chopped

2 garlic cloves, chopped

2 small red chillies, split lengthways and finely chopped

1 pinch freshly grated nutmeg and 1 pinch ground cumin

210g snails blanched, de-shelled and cooked in well flavoured stock

2 tbsp Pernod and 240ml beef stock

550g cooked red kidney beans

60g parsley, finely chopped; salt and black pepper, to taste

Method

Combine 2 tablespoons of the olive oil with the butter in a large frying pan over a medium heat and when frothing add the garlic and shallots. Fry, stirring constantly, until they turn golden brown, then add the chillies, nutmeg, cloves and cumin and cook for 2 minutes more. Add the snails and cook, stirring constantly, for 5 minutes, then add the Pernod and continue cooking until it has all evaporated before adding the beef stock. Now bring the mixture to a boil and continue cooking, stirring all the while, for 3 minutes. Add the beans to the pan along with half the parsley and continue cooking until the beans are just heated through. Take off the heat, stir in the remaining olive oil, then season to taste. Transfer to a serving bowl and add the remaining parsley. Serve immediately with rice.

(Thanks to www.celtnet.org.uk)

8
Cold calling

Each day when I fed and watered the snails I inspected their shells carefully. They had grown much faster than I expected and eventually the first ones showed signs of turning up round the edge like the brim of a hat. They'd reached full size and would soon be ready to sell.

'*To prepare the snails for the table, food must be withdrawn and they should be washed with plenty of water.*' I'd followed the instructions in the book and the moment had come for plunging my little darlings into boiling water.

'Won't you feel like a murderer when you kill them?' friends asked.

It is true that the first time I dropped a bag of snails into boiling water I had to look the other way and hope it was too quick for them to know what was happening. But they didn't scream like lobsters, and neither did I.

It was a hot day and the kitchen was full of steam. I'd cleaned every surface and laid everything out like an operating theatre: fork, knife, chopping boards, cloths and pans. One side of the room was for live snails and the other for cooked. The snails were clean too, inside and out, batched up in drawstring bags to make it easier to pull them out of the boiling water. They bumped around in the pan, filling the air with the smell of damp earth, and I watched the clock to make sure they didn't stay in too long. After exactly five minutes I pulled out the bags and dropped them into a bowl of cold water. There was an art to twisting them out of the shells but soon I had rows of blanched snails in a dish ready to go into the blast freezer. They looked neat, their bodies curled up like pearly little button mushrooms. They would still need to be cooked so I couldn't taste them, but they were undoubtedly beautiful to look at.

I'd been waiting such a long time for this moment to come and I'd worked so hard to get it right that I just collapsed with exhaustion after it was all over. The snails were packed away in the freezer ready to sell.

Cold calling was a bit like going on a blind date. I washed my hair, applied discreet makeup, dressed carefully and practised a winning smile in the mirror. I packed some frozen snails into my smart coolbag, which looked like a laptop case, and lined up a dozen live ones in the net bag I'd sewn the night before. Bridal net was just the thing to keep them contained but still able to breathe and the snails were all neatly tucked up in their shells, sleeping off the previous night's exertions. I tied the string with a bow and put the bag into a cardboard box, then walked down to catch the early bus.

As we swayed along the country lanes, I could feel movement in the box on my knees. To keep my mind occupied I re-read my handout about how to cook them. Under my breath I rehearsed what I was going to say.

'Hello, I'm Helen and I'm a snail farmer.'

No, that sounded too much like a confession to addiction.

'I wondered if you might like to put snails on your menu.' No, that was a bit too tentative. I needed to appear confident.

I glanced round to see if anyone was listening. The bus was full of early shoppers, mostly too deep in conversation to notice, but across the aisle a toddler in a pushchair with a dummy in his mouth was looking up at me curiously. I smiled, he started to cry and his mother glared at me. Thankfully at that moment we swung into the bus station and I made my escape.

I walked nervously down the street holding the box carefully, trying to avoid bumping into people in a hurry. The woman at the counter in the delicatessen smiled as I went in. I put my box down on the counter and mumbled something, my head down as I rummaged in my handbag to find a business card. She called to her boss, who was inhaling his second or third cigarette of the day outside the back door. He dragged himself into the shop and glanced at my card, then sighed deeply and shook his head. He picked up his cup of coffee and wandered away, throwing a reply over his left shoulder: 'Nah. They won't buy nothing like that here.'

She watched him retreat and then turned back to me. 'Don't mind him. He's a grumpy old sod. We just do sandwiches really. It's not that sort of place.' She smiled sympathetically. 'Can I have a look?' I lifted the lid of the cardboard box. Instead of neat rows of tidily tucked snails there was a tangled heap of bodies. They were all climbing over each other to see what was going on and I had to admit they didn't look too appetising. I offered to open the bag but she lifted both her hands to protect herself and stepped back. 'Oh no. There's no need for that.' We both laughed. 'I think the frozen ones would probably be best. Look, you won't sell them here, with old stick in the mud in charge, but give me your card. I know someone who'd be interested, he's head chef at the Bouillabaisse in Whitstable. The DFLs are a bit more adventurous. Go and see Dave and tell him I sent you.'

By the time I got back on the bus and put the box down on my lap the bottom was distinctly damp.

The locals of Whitstable refer to the incomers as DFLs - Down From London - and it's not meant to be a compliment. Whitstable went upmarket after it was featured in a glossy magazine. Smart people started to buy weekend cottages there and consequently the price of houses went through the roof. But they've been good at resisting the powers of destructive change that sought to bring supermarkets into a place where the small shop was still the high street king. They've injected money into the local economy and when it comes to eating they are much more adventurous in their tastes. Although the locals are not keen on the DFL invasion, from my point of view it's definitely a good thing.

From Borstal Hill you can see the boats in Whitstable harbour and smell the sea. The wartime wooden forts on the horizon have been joined by a delicate new forest of windmills. The land around the harbour is below sea level. Locals will tell you about the floods of '63 when those rows of expensively renovated Victorian cottages were under water. Despite re-plastering and painting inside you could see the tidemark on the walls. Tiny shops populate the narrow streets behind the sea wall, each packed with treasure to draw in the passer by: glittering 'must–haves' for magpies. The restaurant Bouillabaisse was squeezed in between them, its courtyard garden entered through wrought iron gates, rusted by the salty wind. As I made my way towards the door, between tables and chairs, vine tendrils from the pergola brushed my hair. Inside it was warm and womb-like, with terracotta walls and low lighting. Fresh hop bines hung from the rafters and the day's specials were written up on the blackboard over a disused kitchen range. It dated from the time when ale was served from ordinary houses in every street to a population wary of drinking the polluted water.

Dave was expecting me and pleased that I'd made the effort to go to see him personally. Fresh out of college, he was young with dark curly hair, like a choir boy in his white kitchen coat. I held out the box of snails and he opened the bag, took one out and turned it upside down. The snail wriggled and waved its antennae at him, then twisted round to examine his fingers, giving them a quick nibble just to see if they were edible. 'Hmm! They look succulent,' said Dave. But I think he was speaking for both of them.

He bought five dozen snails and suggested some other local chefs to try. 'Eddie at The Grand would be a good place to start. Mention my name,' he said, and I walked out onto the street feeling more confident. We had lift off at last.

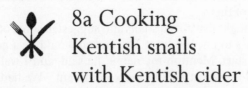

8a Cooking Kentish snails with Kentish cider

Kentish Cider is an essential ingredient in cooking locally grown edible snails and here is how to use it. In true Mrs Beaton style: first catch your snails and let them dry off so that they go into temporary aestivation.

To make your cooking stock:

Ingredients

1 measure cider

10 measures water

1 crushed clove garlic, chopped shallot, chopped carrot

sea salt and black pepper

1 clove, 1 bay leaf, small sprinkling of cinnamon and nutmeg

chopped parsley and thyme (could be dried)

1 whole bird's eye chilli (don't break it up or the stock could be too hot)

(One litre of stock would cook a kilo of snails.)

Method

Make a 10% brine, preferably with sea salt

Bring a large pan of water to rapid boil and add salt. Drop the sleeping snails into the boiling water and bring back to the boil for five minutes. Plunge them into cold water after blanching so that you can handle the shells to remove the snail using a small fork. Twist the snail with the shape of the shell to remove it.

Drop the de-shelled snails into hot brine and boil for thirty minutes to remove slime.

Rinse well.

Drop snails into the hot stock, bring back to the boil and simmer for about one and a half hours. I use a slow cooker for this part of the process so that I can be sure they won't boil dry. At the end of the cooking process turn off the heat and leave in the stock while you prepare the garlic butter.

For the garlic butter:

Ingredients

Per 250g pack unsalted English butter (taken out of the fridge well ahead of time) which should do 4 dozen snails, depending on how much you like garlic butter.

20g chopped garlic

40g chopped shallot

Freshly picked parsley – enough to colour it green

Add cider to taste but try 70ml

Method

The herbs, garlic and shallot are most easily chopped in a food processor with the cider unless you are a skilled chef. Then mix well with the butter.

Drain the snails well and reheat with the cider butter in a hot oven in an oven proof dish until the butter bubbles but don't burn it. Serve with crusty bread and a side salad.

9
Flower and Produce Show

Unless you want to meet a gorilla it's not a good idea to drive down Bourne Lane on August Bank Holiday Monday. For those of us who live within sniffing distance of the zoo it's a day for admiring the length of our runner beans and the size of our pumpkins. It's certainly not a day for getting into a car and joining the pilgrimage to the sea either. In these parts we can watch the sea rolling in and out any time of the year, and enjoy the beach without the crowds. The Flower and Produce Show is a safer bet.

The snails made their first public appearance in the village at the annual show to much marvelling and curiosity. I asked if I could enter them to be judged but the organisers didn't know which category to put them in so they offered me a free table. I dressed the stall with care, covering the table with a gold cloth and hanging varnished shells at eye level.

'Could you keep snails in a rabbit hutch?' The young woman asking the question had been standing silently, watching and listening for some time while I explained how they were kept. It seemed like a strange question but it turned out she operated a sort of Hotel Bunny for small mammals left at home when their owners went away. She'd been threatened by the council with business rates and needed an agricultural activity to keep them at bay. Six empty hutches seemed to offer a unique opportunity, assuming she wasn't expecting the rabbits and snails to co-habit. I imagined the snails having to plough through fur to get to their food and I wondered what rabbits do when they find their lettuce inhabited.

The snails posed for the cameras and looked around curiously. The notice beside them declared: 'Nubile young snails seek ambitious chef for short term relationship'. Lots of children wanted to hold them but their parents were less eager. No chefs materialised and the following year we created less of a stir.

The event is always staged in the 14th century tithe barn next to the church where parishioners used to store their ten per cent tax for the church, the doorways tall and wide for hay wagons to drive through. For this twenty first century harvest the side aisles were occupied by trestle tables laden with the fruits of hard work: not corn but corn dollies, not hops and hay but strawberry jam and patchwork cushions, hand-made cards and wooden jigsaws. Spotlights on the oak beams that supported the thatch picked out the gloss on aubergines and tomatoes waiting to be judged. Pumpkins and cauliflower joined the quest for a prize. Outside, smartly dressed chickens stood in their wire cages looking confused, as would-be competitors hurried past purposefully, carrying baskets and bags. Three geese rushed from one side of a cardboard box to the other, picking up the air of panic. Eventually a rope was firmly placed across the door to exclude latecomers and silence descended. The judges moved about their painstaking work, dissecting the exhibits with a surgeon's care, savouring fragments of Victoria sponge and holding jars of honey up to the light.

Snail racing sounded like a good idea. I set up the race track and a crowd soon gathered. Each child chose a snail to back and gave it a name like Speedy, Lightning or Golden Streak. Thomas had golden hair and carefully chose a snail to match. He whispered advice on strategy before putting his protege on the starting block facing the right way. I said 'Bang!' for the starting gun and Thomas crouched low, calling the name of his favoured runner. "Come on Shelley!" The snails wandered around aimlessly, exploring their surroundings and greeting each other with much bowing and passing of the time of day. Thomas looked up at me as if I might have all the answers. 'How do we get them to go?' he said. We tried laying trails of food to draw them in the right direction but they couldn't seem to understand the rules at all. One by one the children lost interest until I was left on my own with Thomas and the snails. He looked despondent and kicked the table leg before wandering off. I glared at the snails and thought about garlic butter. They carried on with their conversation, oblivious to the athletic expectations that we had of them.

Looking back, Bank Holiday Monday felt as though it would be the last real day of summer. I stood in the garden later, watching the evening arrive early. A late barbecue was getting started in a neighbouring garden but there was no sound drifting across the fields from the zoo. A hedgehog snuffled about in the flower bed and pipistrel bats flew in low between the trees to divebomb the cloud of midges over the pond. After that, I thought, the evenings would begin to draw in fast and by half past four I would be closing the windows against a chilly wind.

Foraging has an honourable history, going as far back into the past as you can imagine. In Kent, where the fields are full of fruit trees and crops, it is hardly surprising that the hedgerows are full of apples, plums, wild hops and cobnuts. Coppicing for fencing has not quite fallen out of favour so sweet chestnuts are still there for the picking. The countryside reflects the past and changes to meet the needs of each age. Not so long ago villagers would harvest local wild food to take home and eat. Perhaps most of us can remember going blackberrying. Now wild food is fashionable and restaurants in London will pay good prices so cottage industries have grown up to supply the demand. Miles was our local forager and I hoped to persuade him to market my snails.

I like to approach Chartham across the Downs so I can look down on the rolling hillsides. In summer the corn is embroidered with poppies below the hedge-line but now the fields have been ploughed, the soil knitted into a tweedy brown sweater for the winter. You can still see the water tower from miles away, marking the spot where the county asylum once stood. The road layout of the new estate still bears the old street names and the red brick nurses' home has been converted into luxury flats. The clock tower on the admission block still overlooks the playing field. It's less imposing surrounded by a modern development but it'll be a long time before the reputation of the place fades.

In the past there were hop fields all round the asylum and near the bottom of the valley the hoppers' huts still stand. They would have been empty at this time of year, but full of pickers in the season. The patients joined in with the picking, and in the old photographs you can't tell which of the pickers were patients, which were staff and which were 'migrant workers', down from London for the summer. All that remains now is the oast houses, long ago detached from their purpose. But the fields of fruit that replaced the hops still attract a moving population of people trying to make a living.

The hospital farm down the hill behind the wards was sold off before the hospital closed, when engaging the patients in farming went out of fashion. When the farm was operating you could approach on foot from Canterbury along the lane through Larkey Valley Wood. There were seven farm cottages in two terraced blocks: a block of four which fronted onto the road, the others behind. The cottages were already empty and decaying when I first saw them some years ago. I drove past many times before curiosity overwhelmed me and I found the courage to look inside. The ground floor of the end cottage, immediately inside the entrance, still had a wooden cart in it but part of the space enclosed a toilet. There was a living room on the other side with a gas geyser, a cast iron range and a tin bath still hanging on the wall: kitchen and bathroom all rolled into one. I imagined that the families who lived there would have spent most of their time in this room when they weren't working on the farm; children worked too, no doubt. Looking out of the window I could see the kitchen overlooked the piggery and I wondered what the smell and flies would have been like in the summer, living so close to the animals. In the yard opposite the cottages was a row of outbuildings where cows were milked, corn was ground and hay stored.

The farm cottages were converted into homes for first time buyers and the outbuildings made workshops for new businesses to grow: catering and furniture restoration. This is where I found the forager.

The entrance to the yard on Cockering Road was between tall brick pillars, which are all that's left now of the high brick wall with spiked railings that surrounded the whole site until the 1960s. When I knocked on the barn door there was a muffled response and as it was opened I put my head inside and called out. The building was divided in two by an upper floor just above head height, reached from an open staircase. A disembodied voice invited me to go up. I picked my way across the ground floor, which was littered with open boxes filled with bunches of greenery and bags of berries. A puffball sat beside piles of cobnuts and sweet chestnuts. The office upstairs was warm and the man himself sat beside his computer screen – I suppose I should have expected technology to have invaded. We talked about living off the land and he admired my snails.

'We used to collect Roman snails but of course we can't do that now they're protected. We search and collect all week, then send out an email newsletter telling chefs what's in season so they can let us know what they want. Then we deliver on Thursdays. If you like we'll let them know they can have snails if they want them and just see what happens.'

As soon as I got home the phone rang.

'Can we get you to talk about eating snails out of the garden?' It was Radio London.

'Is that the only thing you want to talk about?' I asked.

It was.

I sighed. 'I'm not really an expert on wild food. I'm a snail farmer.' I wanted to sell my produce and they want me to promote food for free.

'You told Radio Kent they were the same species so you said, in theory you could eat the wild ones.' That was true… it was a throwaway comment last time I was asked this question which seems to pop into everyone's minds as soon as I mention snails. The next question is often about eating slugs.   'We'd like to slot you in on Monday at 6.20.'

'In the morning?'

'Yes.'

I tried delaying tactics. 'Can I think about it and get back to you?'

'I need to know now, I'm afraid.' She paused just long enough to pile on the pressure and I caved in.

'Okay,' I said. 'Monday it is then … 6.20 … am … live?'

'Live.'

It was Friday evening so I had all weekend to get nervous. I started jotting down notes on Saturday morning. They had their agenda but what did I want to say? I wanted to tell them I had a good product to sell; snails are eaten all over the world but for some reason it's seen as adventurous or disgusting to people in Britain. Lads on a stag night dare each other to eat them while in other places their peers gather snails from the hedgerows to take home and eat with relish. What's so different about cockles and mussels and whelks?

You know what it's like when you're afraid of oversleeping. It was dark the first time I woke with a start. I pressed the light on the clock and discovered it was Monday – but only just. I woke several more times but at 5.30, when the sky was lightening, I gave up the struggle and got up to make a cup of tea. I couldn't take it back to bed in case I fell asleep again so I washed the kitchen floor and started putting things away. I was sitting beside the phone reading through my notes time after time and practising deep breathing when it rang. I could hear the programme in the background and the presenters introducing the topic of beating the credit crunch by eating wild food. After all that anxiety the whole thing only lasted a few minutes but somehow I'd become an expert.

9a Collecting wild snails and cooking them with mushrooms and leeks

Farmed snails are the same species as the common garden snails so it is perfectly feasible to eat the snails out of your garden. But you do need to be sure they haven't eaten anything poisonous. The best way to do that is to keep them in captivity for a couple of weeks. Give them food and water and clean them out each day to make sure they are clean inside. Before I cook them I withdraw food for a few days and give them lots of water to drink. Then let them dry off a little so that they retreat into their shells. That way you get a nice rounded mushroom shape on the plate.

Over the years I've met lots of people from different countries all round the world who told me stories about collecting snails from the wild and taking them home to cook. The countries this happened in ranged from Malta, Cyprus, Greece, Spain, Italy, Eastern Europe, Turkey and West Africa for land snails and as far as the Philippines, where they were freshwater snails. A Maltese woman told me she used to go out first thing in the morning to collect snails for her mother to cook her for breakfast. In different countries it is different species of snail that is eaten

It is curious to think that now snails, like oysters, are seen as a high status food associated with Michelin starred restaurants when they started as food for the poor. Snails, like cockles, winkles and whelks, are an excellent food; a source of protein, minerals and vitamins with little or no stored fat, excellent for the omega threes that we associate with healthy eating. In these times of economic hardship it makes no sense at all to me that there is good food on our doorsteps that people are not using.

Eating snails is part of our cultural heritage. Snails were brought here by the Romans two thousand years ago to eat. They were widely eaten in Britain for centuries afterwards and no one seems to know why they fell off the menu. If they are a nuisance in your garden you only have yourselves to blame – eat them!

Snails with mushroom and leek soup

Ingredients

250g mushrooms, sliced – you can use easily available chestnut mushrooms or if you can get wild mushrooms then use them for this tasty recipe

6 blanched, de-shelled snails

the white part of a leek, washed and chopped

clove or two of garlic, crushed

handful of chopped fresh parsley

tablespoonful of cream for a luxurious texture

small potato, chopped, to thicken the soup

tablespoonful good quality oil to fry

wine or cider

250ml vegetable stock

Method

Fry the garlic, mushrooms and leeks gently in oil, then add the stock with a dash of alcohol, the potato and the snails. Cook slowly for at least an hour.

Make sure the potato is broken up to thicken the soup. Adjust seasoning with salt and black pepper. Stir in the cream and fresh parsley just before serving.

10
A healthy living

I pulled my coat more tightly round me and leaned against the wind as I walked down the hill past the church towards the river. Children were bursting out of school, running down the alley and erupting onto Jubilee Field. Soon the slide would be polished clean and the swings squeaked to exhaustion. I listened for traffic before crossing the street and slipping down into the sheltered space between the houses to the narrow wooden bridge. It was a quiet retreat when I needed to think. Leaning on the handrail, I could look down into the water at clouds of small fish in the fast-flowing current. The millwheel behind me created eddies and ripples but somehow the fish held themselves steady, fins flickering faster than I could see. A family of ducks prospected in the shallows under the trees, tipping upside down, feet in the air, to forage along the reedy bank and amongst the watercress. I'd often caught the flash of a kingfisher here, but not today. Today was not a good day. I was worried about the snails. I was also having trouble getting help, which added to my worry.

The vet's receptionist laughed. 'For a moment there I thought you said you were farming snails.'

'I am.'

She laughed again. 'Well, I've never come across that before.'

I was getting a bit tired of being the source of merriment for so many women who answered the phone for a vet.

'I don't think Alan can help you,' she continued. 'He won't know anything about that sort of thing.'

It seemed no one could help. I had even phoned Devon but it seemed that ownership of the snail farm there had changed and I didn't get a very friendly reception from Frank's successors.

Each day, the pile of dead bodies grew higher.

Saturday 14th: 13 dead

Sunday 15th: 6 dead

Monday 16th: 17 dead

My record book told the grim tale. I didn't have a clue what was going wrong. My beautiful breeding snails looked absolutely fine the night before and yet in the morning there would be more bodies to account for and dispose of. Why was it that a plump healthy looking snail turned its metaphorical toes up overnight? I couldn't tell if it was the food, the water, the temperature or just old age. Perhaps they had caught something nasty. I disinfected their home, inspected the food for mould and changed the water. Maybe they were just thirsty? These land snails liked a bowl of water. The babies climbed straight in and played Loch Ness monsters, skimming along the bottom with their heads sticking out. On a warm day the big ones looked like they were relaxing in a hot tub, with their bodies underwater and their heads draped languorously over the side.

I had grown fond of them and it appeared the feeling was mutual. The way they stuck their heads up over the edge of the box to look round when I took the lid off to feed them was quite endearing. They made a moist noise when they moved about and when they ate it sounded like a cat lapping milk. They nibbled my fingers very gently when I picked them up, exploring every pore and wrinkle. I cleaned out and fed the snails every day for months on end so of course I grieved if they got squashed or crept into a corner and died.

I couldn't carry on like this. I needed someone to tell me why the snails were dying. I started searching the net for vet labs, emailing one at random to ask if they would do a post mortem for me, but they made it clear they wouldn't deal direct with the public, only with a vet. So I started phoning vets. I wasn't going to call him out every time one of them looked a bit peaky but this was an emergency. I scoured the Yellow Pages, trying every name on the list, but they were all too busy or not interested.

'Well, you could try Mr Stewart,' said one of the only helpful women I spoke to. 'I know he deals with some exotic pets.' She gave me his number but this time I wanted to go for the face to face approach as phoning didn't seem to produce the desired result. I looked at the clock. It was quite late in the afternoon so I flew out of the house, threw my bags into the car and raced along the country lanes as fast as I dared, hoping I wouldn't meet a tractor.

I'd got the address but the roads weren't named and it was a place I'd never been to before. Eventually I pulled the car into a space and abandoned it. 'Excuse me,' I said, approaching a woman hurrying along the pavement with a pushchair and a golden retriever on a lead. 'I noticed you've got a pet so I wondered if you would know where the vet was.' The dog looked up and smiled at me and his owner pointed down a side street. There it was, tucked away in a parade of village shops.

According to the opening hours on the door it had closed half an hour ago. I sighed and turned away, thinking I'd have to come back. Then I heard voices and decided to give the door a push.

'I'm sorry. We're closed now till tomorrow morning.'

'Oh dear. I was afraid I'd missed the boat.'

The receptionist looked at me sympathetically. 'Was

it urgent?'

'I really only wanted access to the labs.' I made good eye contact with her and she listened carefully. Vets seemed to fall into categories according to the animals they would see: small animals, farms, horses or exotics. If they were used to dealing with small furry things then they might not know one end of a gecko from the other. This guy was South African so I hoped he might have a wider perspective and at last I struck gold. He not only agreed to take us on but didn't charge me a fee. He said he probably didn't know any more about snails than I did but he might learn something new.

The morning I was due to go back to the vet I searched for a snail that looked as though it was still breathing but had lost interest in life. The poor thing was lying on its side in the corner so I lifted it out and put it into a travelling box. Sitting in the vet's surgery was a curious experience. The dogs and cats seemed to know that disagreements were not allowed on these premises and called a truce. A golden retriever lay with his head on his paws watching the comings and goings. His owner spoke to him quietly each time the door opened and closed in case he made a dash for freedom. Frantic scrabbling of claws came from a plastic carrying case on the floor beside him and the end of a pink nose sniffed the air through the holes from time to time. Whatever it was could probably smell the Jack Russell struggling on its owner's lap opposite, desperate to get down on the floor. Owners and pets passed the time of day, swapped the latest news and compared notes on the neighbours.

The vet took samples from my very sick snail and sent them off in the post. A couple of weeks later I was charged an extortionate amount of money for a post mortem which told me the labs really had no idea what it had died of. The report pointed out that the specimen was infested with bacteria, as a slightly rotting snail would be, and perhaps antibiotics might help.

I wasn't keen to use chemicals but I talked it over with

the vet and decided to give it a try. The chosen remedy was normally given to pigs and he had to guess the dilution. How much smaller than a pig is a snail? I went home with an ampoule in my pocket. I diluted the liquid into a bottle and sprayed them with it tentatively, grateful that I didn't have to administer pills or injections. Then I sat back and waited.

It didn't kill them, which had been my first fear. It didn't seem to make their eyes water or irritate their delicate skins and the rate of mortality did seem to slow down a bit. But they weren't laying eggs and that was serious. My "crop", so to speak, was going to run out.

It was spring, when a young snail's fancy should lead to looking for a mate and laying eggs. Our breeding stock wandered around ignoring each other. We thought we had the temperature and lighting to their liking but nothing seemed to work. What do you do when snails just stuff themselves full of food, then roll over and go back to sleep?

Throwing stones in the sea is very therapeutic. I crunched along the beach, climbing the wooden groynes, delighting in the muted greens and greys and steely blues of the scene that suited my mood. I picked up a flat stone and leaned back to throw it low along the water with a flick of the wrist that made it spin. It touched the water's surface for a moment before rising up and back down again, almost noiselessly. Searching for the smooth oval pebbles that would bounce in that satisfying way uncovered mussel shells, mermaids' purses and seaweed smells. Next time I threw, a fast moving lurcher suddenly appeared, racing through the surf. He plunged straight into the sea and reappeared a few moments later carrying something in his mouth. He ran over to me, showering me with water, and dropped his find at my feet. I looked down at his driftwood treasure, the pleading eyes and his rear end wagging vigorously.

'Hello,' I said. 'Where did you come from?'

He sprung up and barked, leaping backwards and forwards with excitement.

'Spider!' A figure in the middle distance was calling him. He turned and then looked up at me and down at his find, as though he was trying to make up his mind what to do.

'Come on, Spider!'

'Go on! Off you go!' I said, pointing to where his owner stood. He grabbed the driftwood and bounded away, clearing the breakwaters easily.

The clouds were moving fast across the sky and it was starting to rain but there was a tiny smudge of blue on the horizon. Perhaps there was still hope that my business wasn't going to slowly die before my eyes.

The phone was ringing as I opened the front door. I dropped everything and ran to catch it before it stopped.

'Hello?' I gasped

'Hello there! You sound like you've been running!'

It was Sarah.

'What's happened?'

I sighed. 'Everything just seems to be going wrong.'

'Everything? Or just the snails?'

'The snails.' At this point they were everything to me. 'The breeders keep dying … and they're not laying eggs … and I don't know what to do.'

'Can't you ask that guy in Devon for advice?'

'No … he's sold up and left the country.'

'Oh, I see! He sells you this wonderful business idea and then emigrates.'

'Well, if you put it like that I suppose it doesn't sound great. But it's been going so well up to now. I've got customers who want to buy them and I've nursed lots of babies to full size and sold them.' I looked at my hands, noticing the dirt and broken nails. Farmer's hands. 'I really felt I was getting somewhere.'

'And how much money did he say you could make?'

'Well, he generalised quite a lot, but he said he sold 32,000 snails in his first month of trading.'

'And how much profit was he making?'

'Well, he wasn't specific about his turnover ... but you couldn't expect him to give that away. It's commercially sensitive information.'

'But you must have got some idea how much you could make.'

'Well, I got this business plan from him showing how to make £30,000 a year.'

'I wonder why he sold up then?'

'He did say something about relatives abroad that he wanted to join.'

Sarah didn't say anything. I felt myself suddenly rise out of the sludge of self pity. 'Look, there are hundreds of family snail farms in France. If they can make it work then why can't I?'

I could almost hear Sarah grinning. 'Then let's go and find out how they do it.'

10a Lent and farming snails in Eastern Europe

Snail farming is big business in many Eastern European countries and has been since the boom in the eighties. The advantage that they have is cheaper land and a low paid labour force. The result from where I sit is lots of emails from companies who have produced tons of edible snails available at a low price and are looking for a contact in the UK to manage their export business.

I discovered recently that snails are associated with Lent amongst orthodox Christians in Cyprus and in Prague and also with the pre-Christmas period which in the past would have had similar associations with fasting. This makes an interesting link with the history of snail farming in the UK. Monasteries are one of the places where there is evidence of snail farming dating back centuries. One of the reasons for this is thought to be that monks were not supposed to eat meat at certain times such as Lent. They called snails 'wallfish', and by defining them as 'fish' they felt able to put them on the menu when they were fasting.

We have no recipes particularly associated with monasteries but perhaps they used this one that dates from the eighteenth century:

To Stew Snails

Scour them, and cleanse them well, put them into a Pipkin (pan) with Claret and Wine-vinegar, Salt, Pepper, Mace, grated Bread, Thyme shred, Capers, and the Yolks of a hard Egg or two, minced. Stew all these together, then put in a good piece of Butter, and shake them well together, warm a Dish, rub it with a Clove of Garlick, lay Sippets (croutons?) in the Dish, put on the Snails, garnish with Barberries and slices of Lemon.

(The Cook's and Confectioner's Dictionary (1723) John Nott) (re-published with thanks to Janet at The Old Foodie, www.the oldfoodie.com)

11
Week thirteen

Naked black branches pierced a clear blue sky as we drove to the port and the sun burnt my arm through the window. You would never have known it was March. Dover was quiet, no queues of tourists, but a steady stream of lorries poured past us into the hold of the ferry, filling the central space before we sneaked into a narrow gap along the edge. The café was almost empty and overnight drivers stretched out along the soft benches were already settling to sleep. The three of us kept our voices low so as not to wake them. The ship was almost motionless in its passage across the channel.

Driving on the wrong side of the road was easier with Sarah as navigator because she could translate the signs at the junctions and tell me which way to go. Leaving the main route, we made our way along steeply cambered narrow roads, above fields without hedges, denuded of crops, through whitewashed villages.

'The place looks deserted,' I said. 'Do you think anyone actually lives here?'

'France is closed for lunch.'

'It's difficult to believe it's a working day.' The long straight road stretched ahead of us for mile after endless mile. 'Where on earth is this place? Do you think we've gone past it?'

'No, there it is.' Rebecca pointed to a small hand-painted sign on the side of a low building. 'L'escargotiere. Is that how you say it?'

'Like cafetiere,' said Sarah.

The fingerpost pointed along an even narrower lane.

'Look at that awful road surface. Have I really got to take my poor car down there?' I looked aghast at the worn surface, so dotted with craters it was hard to believe it had ever been tarmacked.

I took the turning and rolled slowly downhill, trying to judge whether each pothole was wider than our wheelbase, while Rebecca and Sarah looked from left to right, inspecting each shuttered house carefully for telltale signs.

The farm gate, when we finally found it, was clearly marked and a school bell dangled invitingly above it. A few moments after the nostalgic sound rang out across the yard, Pierre emerged from behind a barn, hair blowing in the wind, black clothes flapping round his wiry frame and chickens scattering from under his boots. He threw open the gate and invited us in with a smile. I had tried to imagine what he would be like from our tortured email conversations. My written French had improved a lot since he'd first got in touch and issued an invitation but I still couldn't speak it easily. Rebecca was never a linguist. Sarah, however, was fluent in French because of her childhood spent abroad and she became immediately animated. I had never heard her speak so much. They chattered away like old friends. For a while I tried to follow the conversation but Rebecca's face glazed over quite quickly and eventually I gave up too. A white farmhouse faced the yard, sheltered on two sides by brick and wood outbuildings, held together by years of creosote. From an open door we could hear the rumble of a refrigeration unit and smell last year's snails in storage. On the other side was the shop and kitchen block, more recently built of white painted breeze blocks. The kitchen was whitewashed inside as well as out and kitted out in stainless steel like an operating theatre. A large cauldron stood each side of a white stone sink with its boiler above. We sniffed the jars of spices and herbs and talked about poaching and simmering, about texture and flavour.

'Apparently he's met a lot of French people who've had a bad experience with badly cooked snails,' Sarah said.

In the second room, a stainless steel autoclave reinforced the air of the hospital. Three big chest freezers held snails prepared in dozens of different ways: in shells or out, with butter and cheese or Pernod and cassis. We compared notes on prices – the fall of the pound against the euro – and Sarah translated with apparent ease.

Outside, a black pot-bellied pig grunted a welcome and came forward to lean against the fence for her head to be scratched. Two goats gazed into the far distance while chewing thoughtfully, carrying on with life as though we were not there at all. The holding was split into paddocks, each with a few animals, the boundary marked by a hedge.

There was a pause in the conversation and Sarah turned to me. 'Pierre is saying that he opens in the evenings in the summer so people can come and see the snails being watered and fed. When tourists come to visit they like to see the other animals too. It makes more of an outing while they look and listen. He said he thinks that if they are enjoying themselves they are more likely to buy snails when they get to the shop.'

I looked across at him and nodded and smiled to show I understood. The main enclosure for the fattening season was like an enormous fruit cage, netted to protect the crop from birds of prey. I tried to imagine the long summer evenings when artificial rain falls after each hot dry day and the snails come out for a promenade, an alfresco buffet and the all night party. A white hob ferret had been appointed night watchman. As soon as he heard us coming he rushed to intercept, sniffing the air and regarding us with suitable suspicion. He demanded that we declare our intentions so I bent down to his level and explained. He seemed to understand my English perfectly, accepting my explanation, then scampered off to check the boundary for intruders. Pierre said that rats find snails irresistible but the ferret keeps them away.

In the laying shed, ardent snails pursued one another with amorous intent, heads high. They signalled to each other in snail semaphore, antennae at a jaunty angle like the feathered fascinator on a wedding guest. The subdued lighting lent an air of the nightclub; a sense of occasion to the couplings. Clumps of pearly white eggs reflected the light in the warm humid air. It was week thirteen of the year, when the breeders came in from the cold to begin the cycle again.

We sat in the airy kitchen drinking tea while Sarah reminisced about her childhood holidays travelling the globe and Pierre told us about how he had gone into farming as something completely different after several difficult years as a social worker with asylum seekers trying to reach England through the port.

In my halting French I couldn't express all my hopes and dreams to Pierre, but eventually we gave him our thanks and said our goodbyes before heading off towards the channel.

The boat was full of commuters, trailing back home to Kent at the end of a normal working day in a different country.

'That must feel strange,' I said. 'But I guess you can get used to anything if it happens every day.'

Sarah didn't reply but then she leaned forward. 'So was the visit useful?'

'I think so,' I said. 'It was good to see a snail farm actually working. I need to think about what I've learnt but it's given me some ideas.' I turned to Rebecca. 'What do you think?'

'It was difficult to take it all in. I think I missed a lot of what he said because of the language barrier.'

'Well, it wasn't easy, but he must be doing something

right as you could see those breeders were definitely laying eggs. What do you think about his idea of opening to the public?' I asked.

'Well, it would be a lot of work,' Rebecca said. 'It's not something I'd want to do. The horses are my first priority.'

'What about all that cooking?' said Sarah.

'I got the impression he enjoyed the cooking better than the farming,' I said.

'Have you got space for a commercial kitchen like that?' asked Sarah.

'Not really,' I said, looking round at our fellow travellers, exhausted from their long day at work. 'More important really is my feeling that I don't want to spend all my life in the kitchen. I like cooking but not enough to want to make my living that way. It's farming – growing things and looking after animals – that gives me pleasure.'

Over the months that followed we thought a lot about what we'd seen. Pierre and I may have shared some of the same experiences but we had different motivations. The visit had shown us that snail farming was a viable proposition and planted the seed of an idea in my mind.

11a Farming and cooking snails in France

If we look back to the historical roots we find that snail farming became more commercial in the Middle Ages with thousands of snails raised in the Swiss Alps being sent down the Danube to Vienna and beyond. It became established as a business enterprise in France during the latter part of the eighteenth century. French wine merchants who went to Burgundy each year were served snails collected from the local vineyards and soon they were being sent to restaurants in Paris. At the beginning of the season the first baskets of snails were brought to the Parisian markets by specially hired coaches, rather like the first prized bottles of Bordeaux. By 1850 the coming of the railway meant that snails could be transported greater distances so new markets developed across France, Italy and Spain. Many other countries have entered snail farming in recent years, including Belgium, Germany, Romania, Macedonia, Serbia, Montenegro, Croatia, Bosnia, Poland, the Czech Republic and Bulgaria.

Hundreds of French family farms produce snails out of doors during the summer season for the local and tourist market. There are also factories producing canned, frozen and bottled snails with a variety of different garnishes. There are still some people who collect snails from the wild but life has changed in France, as it has everywhere else, and French cooks also go to the supermarket to buy ready prepared food.

Varying the recipe

The basic procedure for cooking snails remains the same but after that you can let your imagination run riot. Begin by blanching your snails, boiling them in brine and then slow cooking for at least an hour and twenty minutes (see Kentish cider recipe for details). To the cooked snails you add a garnish which is often garlic and parsley butter. This is said to be associated with the Burgundy region. But the flavour of the usual herb and garlic butter can be varied by the addition of cheeses or alcohol. The butter can be replaced with oil or duck fat. The herbs used can be varied, for example, by using thyme or chervil, which has an aniseed flavour. Or you could add ground walnuts.

Cooked snails are often served in presentation shells of a different species called Helix lucorum.

These are collected from the wild and prized for the attractiveness and uniformity of their shells. If you buy tinned snails they are often sold with a stack of empty shells, and those shells are from Helix lucorum. You can put the snails back into the shells they came out of, provided you are confident they are clean and assuming they are not damaged. As an alternative you could serve them in pastry cases, profiteroles or vol au vents for that truly retro seventies look.

12
Strawberries, ferrets and the summer solstice

It was dawn in the village orchard on the longest day of the year. It had been a warm night and you could drown in the heavy scent from the strawberry fields. A narrow beam of light cut through the circle at the top of a totem pole. Carved hands reached up the oak wood, pressing into the grain. An alien army of rusty metal sculptures crouched in the long grass. A papier mache bag lady slumped on the bench. A huge model rabbit leaned up against an apple tree and inside-out stuffed teddy bears hung from the branches, their red patent shoes shining like ripe fruit. The exhibition was ready.

I'd woken early, unable to sleep for the weight of things to do pressing in on my mind. I'd decided to send an email newsletter to all the local pubs and restaurants asking them if they would want to buy. There were thousands of baby snails to clean out. I needed to order some more snail food and there were lots of email enquiries to deal with. I wrote it all down and left it on my desk before walking out into the bright new day to clear my head.

By noon the sun was hot again and it was Open Gardens in the village. This was the annual chance to go and visit friends whose scented flower beds and neat vegetable patches I already knew; to meet new people who had taken over old gardens and brought them back to life with winding paths, new ponds and fresh vistas. It was a good mix of the familiar and the unknown. The walls of a square-fronted house that I'd walked past so many times surprised me by curving away as I went round to the back. I found it had been a working oast in the nineteenth century and the garden was decorated with Victorian glass bottles retrieved during excavation.

Pots of tea and scones invited passers-by into the big house to admire the formal lawns, rose beds and avenue of limes.

'She doesn't do all this herself, you know,' a neighbour whispered in my ear. 'She's got an army of gardeners and doesn't know one end of a spade from the other.' Walking round in gardening gloves with a trug over one's arm and a pair of secateurs didn't make one a real gardener.

The padlocked gates of the allotments were open for the day, the plots dressed in their Sunday best, festooned with glowing redcurrants. Groups of people wandered along the green paths admiring asparagus beds, teepees of beans and regiments of onions. Chickens scratched about clucking contentedly and gardeners strutted up and down looking equally pleased with themselves. I wandered up and down the rows wondering what they would say if I asked for a plot to grow vegetables for the snails. I went to the organiser's table and asked about the rules for keeping animals on allotments.

'Keeping livestock on allotments is governed by the Allotments Act,' he said sternly. 'You can keep chickens without special permission and since the war we've been able to raise rabbits, though I don't know anyone who does. What did you have in mind?'

When he'd finished laughing we had a long discussion about whether snails could really be classified as livestock. But I persisted and eventually he wrote my name down and told me I'd have to write to the Parish Council because they administered the site. I got the impression I might have difficulty getting it past the allotment committee.

'So how's it going?' Sarah looked at me searchingly over her cup.

'Okay, I think.' I looked round the café at the shoppers resting their feet under the wrought iron tables, bulging bags leaning against each chair. 'Looks like the farmers' market's done well this morning.'

'And you?'

I grinned. She wasn't going to let me off that easily. 'It's been a funny old morning really.' I sat and thought for a moment. I had made the mistake of putting some snails into a strawberry punnet, which had seemed the ideal container: the right size, with holes so they could breathe. By the time I got to the Grand the stupid things had put their heads through the holes and got stuck. Eddie the chef came gallantly to the rescue by cutting round the holes to let them out. I looked at Sarah. 'The chef I met this morning described the snails as cute.'

She raised her eyebrows. 'Not quite the word I would have used but it depends on your point of view, I suppose.'

'You wouldn't believe some of the things people say. I mean, this is a man who despatches mussels, lobsters and crabs without a second thought. But he positively cooed over my snails. He said: "When you come back you'll probably find we haven't cooked them at all but given them all names and toys to play with. Do you think they'd use one of those wheels like hamsters have?"'

Sarah laughed. 'Sounds like you deserve a medal for services to vegetarianism. Is anybody actually eating them?'

'Yes, I've got a few customers and I thought I'd have a go at farmers' markets. I was having a look round this morning. I think I could do it without too much outlay. I wouldn't have the same overheads as a shop but I'd have to sell them hot and ready to eat, I think.' I moved my chair to let a pushchair past.

'So they're laying now, are they, and growing alright?' asked Sarah.

'Yes, they seem fine. Maybe I've finally got the hang of it.'

'Was it the visit to France?'

'Yes, that definitely helped. I think it's got a lot to do with the weather.' I looked down at my empty cup. '... and I can't do much about that.' I looked out at the awnings flapping in the wind. 'It also made me wonder about exporting, as the people of East Kent don't seem overjoyed at this new opportunity I'm offering them. There's a big trade fair in Belgium next March and it looks like the City Council might fund a few of us to go if we want to.'

'Oh yes, you must. I'd leap at the chance if it was me.'

I looked at the clock. 'Actually I've got to go ... sorry! I've got to see a man about a ferret.'

'As you do!'

I laughed and stood up.

'Before you go ...' Sarah put out a hand to stop me. 'I just wondered if you'd done anything about getting a website yet?'

I'd had a quote but it was such a lot of money that I wasn't sure what to do. I'd thought about setting up a

Facebook page or writing a blog because they're free, but I wasn't sure how to talk about the business without giving away too many secrets or exposing my customers to ridicule.

'Not yet.' I pulled my scarf round my neck, started to do up my coat and changed the subject. 'I took the snails into a Brownie group last week.'

'I bet they loved that.'

'They did! And it was such fun… it made me feel like a kid again. The uniforms had changed but the leader was still called Brown Owl and the grown up helpers all had rabbit names from Watership Down.' We both laughed. 'Look, I really must go… it's lovely to see you.'

'Don't let me keep you from your ferretty friends.' Sarah smiled and waved as I left. 'And do something about that website!'

The small furry bundle in my hands nuzzled around my palm looking for a teat, then closed his pink eyes and went back to sleep with his creamy white head resting across my index finger. Although he was only six weeks old his body odour was definitely male.

'It's the smell that keeps the rats away,' his owner said. 'Have you decided what to call him?'

'It has to be something beginning with F to go with ferret,' I said.

'What about Freddie?'

So that's how he got his name. Freddie's father was altogether more business-like in his approach to life. When offered a strawberry, he pounced on it, picking it up firmly by the stalk and giving it a good shake to make sure its neck was broken. Then he dropped it and stood over it, yellow back arched, waiting for it to try and escape. He didn't stay still for long, leaping and dancing round his pen, rolling over, jumping at shadows and noticing every movement and sound around him. He didn't eat until he was sure the sport was over and the fruit had given up the ghost.

Perhaps it was the magic of the summer solstice or the powerful effects of cuddling a warm furry body but I imagined myself with my own plot growing food for the snails and me. In my mind's eye I could see my ground laid out with rows of green vegetables and Freddie leaping about in the foliage, chasing his own shadow.

Dusty arrived two weeks later, beguiling me with her sooty eye makeup and brown paws, like a miniature panda. She was younger and much smaller so I was concerned when Freddie grabbed her by the scruff of the neck at their first meeting. They rolled over and over using all four feet and two sets of teeth to establish who was in charge. He bit her ear when she had the temerity to eat from his bowl but Dusty planted both feet firmly in the bowl and shoved him aside with her shoulder. I could see she wasn't going to stand any nonsense from him. When she'd finished eating his dinner and sampled the water from his bottle, she skipped away down the gangplank into the run with Freddie in hot pursuit. She lured him into a piece of drainpipe, sitting with her nose just peeping out, dark eyes shining wickedly while he hesitated. Dusty waited until he took his courage in both paws and followed her in, before she whipped round and bit him on the nose. Freddie shot out backwards and retreated to a safe distance to recover his dignity. Within a short time they had rearranged the furniture in their nesting box, to the accompaniment of plenty of cursing and swearing on both sides, but after that a few tufts of fur blowing around the lawn were all that remained as evidence of their disagreement.

12a Training for chefs and snails with fish

Craig Mather is a chef lecturer at East Kent College, Broadstairs. He won Student of the Year when he studied at Thanet College (now East Kent College) and also won the Association Culinaire Française National Escoffier Challenge 2005. He told me that as a student he had cooked in some of the best eateries in the country: Le Manoir aux Quat' Saisons, Chewton Glen, Auberge du Lac, Sharrow Bay, Ynyshir Hall and Mallory Court. After qualifying he spent four years at one-starred Mallory Court under the leadership of Simon Haigh before moving back to Kent after starting a family. When I first met him he was Head Chef at Eddie Gilberts, Ramsgate, a fishmongers that built a restaurant within the premises using the abundant fresh local fish available round this coast. There he sometimes used snails as a garnish for fish and this is one of his recipes:

Kentish Plaice & Snails with Capers, Wild Garlic & Pickled Onions Rings

Ingredients

2 x 600g+ plaice

4 vine cherry tomatoes

2 large pickled onions

20 braised snails

2 tbsp capers

12 wild garlic leaves

125g butter

1 tbsp chopped parsley

½ lemon

Method

Braise the snails as for Kentish snails in cider.

Fillet the plaice, skin then place back in to fridge.

Place a non stick frying pan and a small saucepan of boiling water onto the stove.

Slice the onions into 3mm thick slices, then divide into rings.

Quarter the tomatoes and wash the wild garlic.

Chiffonade (finely shred) the parsley.

Season the plaice, then put 2 tbsp of oil into the frying pan. When hot slide the fillets in carefully and cook for 2 minutes on a high heat until golden.

Add the butter and turn the fish carefully over, add the tomatoes, lemon juice, capers, snails and parsley. Keep basting the fillets with this buttery sauce for a further minute.

Blanch the garlic for 30 seconds and then start to plate by arranging the fish onto a plate and dress with the garlic, tomatoes, snails and onion rings. Finish by spooning over the buttery sauce.

Craig says he always liked the idea of teaching the next generations of chefs and when a position became available at the college for a lecturer he jumped at the chance. At East Kent College the catering courses have undoubtedly contributed to Kent's growing reputation as a foodie place but also nationally and worldwide. Notable names to come from the college are:

Gary Rhodes – TV chef & restaurateur

Nathan Outlaw – 2 Michelin star chef

Richard Phillips – Chef & restaurateur

Mark Stubbs – Wheelers, Whitstable

Allan Pickett – Head Chef, Plateau, London

Paul Bates - Executive Chef, Intercontinental, London

Mick Kitts – Training School, Dubai

Jason Brotherton – Executive Chef, Hilton Group, Abu Dhabi

'It is great to see the students' progress while they are on their course and to see them completing personal aims that they have set themselves. We have started to really push again at students competing in competitions.'

13
Exploring the web

The cold hotel conference room was full of men and women looking uncomfortable in their smart suits. The speaker on e-commerce, by contrast, had gone for the dress-down Friday look: baseball cap and Boston University sweatshirt, just in case we were in any doubt of his origins. He began by explaining that Canada is not the same as America and they are both big places compared to the UK. 'Just because your Aunty Ginny lives in the US of A, I wouldn't necessarily know her,' he joked. We smiled indulgently. On the desk in front of him was a soft toy which he picked up and waved at us. 'This is an example of the power of online selling.' Apparently it was supposed to be a clockwork guinea pig, but it looked more like an orange chinchilla, because it had furry ears. Perhaps it was made by someone who had never seen a real one. I couldn't imagine wanting one, except you wouldn't have to feed it or clean it out each day.

Before telling us the rest of the soft toy story he enlarged on his own achievements. He expanded on his theory of the entrepreneur as someone who pushes themselves to the limit. He had run across the desert and roller bladed a marathon, revelling in endurance sports. He liked to try new things, push them as far as he could and then move on to the next thing. He emphasised that he had bought all the gear online and sold it again afterwards without losing a penny on the deal. He had a prestigious job and wanted us to know. He used himself to illustrate that you don't need special characteristics to achieve: he was short, fat and bald; not athletic at all.

'Now let's take the iPhone,' he said. 'Its success rests on how important it was to show everyone you've got one.' He talked about living with a teenage son who sent him emails about what he wanted for his birthday. It made perfect sense if he was never at home; always out of the house, running up the nearest mountain. And that was where the clockwork guinea pig came in. His son had sent him an email to say he wanted one for his birthday. It was the latest "must have" amongst his peers. Although there were plenty about on eBay, he predicted they would soon be selling like hot cakes and by Christmas you wouldn't be able to get one for love nor money. What fools we are to be so easily led to the slaughter, I thought as I left, wondering if I'd really learn anything else useful about selling snails online.

Buying online, on the other hand, I knew all about. If I wanted to keep the flow of baby snails coming I needed some more breeders. That took me back to the Istituto Internazionale di Elicicoltura di Cherasco in Italy. It was my lucky day: they had just translated their snail breeding manual into English.

The snail breeding manual opened my eyes to a whole new method of agriculture. A snail crawled across the front cover and behind it the picture showed what looked like vineyards on a hillside. But those knitted hillsides were open air snail farms. The annual cycle was set out clearly with planting of feedcrops early in the year and 'sowing' of fields with breeding snails in the spring, just as though they were plants. As the snails grew through the year they were collected and sold until the autumn, when they would hibernate. Then we got to the interesting bit: cooking snails the Italian way. We relied on the pictures to tell the story as the text was largely incomprehensible. The bright picture with checked tablecloth, pan of prepared escargots and live snails crawling beside them would have given our Environmental Health Officer heart failure. But the "recepies" were something else. It seemed they could be cooked with bacon, rare mushrooms, cheeses or anchovies. We had fillings for ravioli and stuffings for quail; sauces with wine, vegetables and tomatoes; and feasts involving pastries, polenta or pasta of all shapes and sizes. The possibilities beyond garlic butter were amazing. The manual confidently asserted that molluscs returned from their rural roots to their honourable place at the forefront of gastronomy at the beginning of the nineteenth century. Each year 600 Italian towns hosted festivals to celebrate snail gastronomy.

Rebecca and I talked long and hard about what we should do because it was going to cost a lot, but we decided to take the risk. Without this investment the business was going nowhere. I sent my first email in English asking for a few hundred breeding snails and hoped for the best. The reply took a bit of deciphering:

Dear sir, We communicate you that we exclusively work with quantitative commercial and professional. Then the least one of consignment of reproducers Helix Aspersa is of 2.000 subjects. i'm sorry for my English. If you want a reproducers of HELIX ASPERSA MAXIMA we have a lot of reproducers but you must know that the costs of the transport are very expensive becose we must send you a snail by plane. I thing around € 500,00.

Maria

My Italian was worse than Maria's English and I could see it was going to be quite difficult to communicate. Schoolgirl Latin wasn't going to get me very far. The reply conjured up an image of snails lining up at the airport check in and sliding through the scanner one at a time to check they weren't carrying explosives.

'Wouldn't you have to notify DEFRA if you're importing live animals?' Sarah asked. Well, how would I know? Nobody ever mentioned that on the Archers.

It's not the sort of topic that comes up in other people's everyday conversation with friends. I rushed to the computer and notified DEFRA. They emailed back a whole lot of documents to wade through which told me we could only import from a reputable dealer and the snails needed a veterinary certificate. I tried to picture an Italian vet checking their health. Perhaps he had to pick up each one in turn to test its reflexes and put a tiny thermometer in its mouth. The last leaflet referred us to Appendix A: The List of Prohibited Animals. Molluscs, it seemed, were prohibited imports on the grounds of being potential agricultural pests, except African land snails for domestic pets. I made a frantic call to the man at DEFRA who dealt with prohibited pests.

'Prohibited?' he said. 'Are they? I didn't know that. What list was that, did you say? I wonder who wrote that. I don't think I've ever seen it. Well, it doesn't make much sense, does it? Leave it with me and I'll do some checks at this end.' I left it with him and half an hour later he phoned back to say it was okay and would I email Appendix A to him please so he could get it changed.

Dear Helene, we must wait 3/4 days for the sanitary certificate after we will make a reservation on plain and than we advise you the day that arrive the snails.

Maria

Well she'd almost got my name right so we were making progress. That was the last we heard until I came home late one hot Saturday evening, tired and hungry, to find two messages on the phone.

'This is Gatwick Airport. We've had a consignment of snails here since Thursday. Can you phone back urgently please to tell us when they will be collected?'

Gatwick seemed a long way away but the animal holding shed was staffed round the clock so I had time to eat before leaving. I put on some music and tried to relax as I drove, singing at the top of my voice as I made my way there, with the windows wide open to stay awake. There were lots of interested questions from the smiling staff who helped transfer the enormous cardboard box to the back of my very small car. It took two of us to lift it but somehow it went in.

I drove back carefully in the dark along the motorway. It was nearly midnight by the time we arrived home but the snails had to be unpacked to make sure they were okay. The box was double layered and secured with miles of parcel tape. Inside were four green onion sacks full of completely dry snails. They would be okay to leave until morning. I stood in the doorway for a moment before switching off the light. In the stillness the sacks moved almost imperceptibly, making a very faint rustling sound like shuffling through autumn leaves.

The care instructions that came with them were in Italian but I worked out that water was required to wake them up. Each one was washed carefully and put into the rearing boxes; then they needed a dish of water and some food. It seemed they woke with an overwhelming need to go exploring. Over the next few days I spent a lot of time retrieving snails from the walls and ceiling and putting them back into boxes after they'd pushed off the lids and wandered off. The door stayed shut at night but had to be opened carefully in the morning in case they were on the floor behind it. But mostly they didn't go far, just sticking themselves onto the outside of their own box or the one next door. Perhaps they were looking for their friends and relations. Often in the morning rows of snails would be lined up on the top edge of their boxes, peeping out under the lids, looking down and waving their antennae at me. They were used to a free range life so living in a box must have seemed a bit strange at first. A lot took several applications of water to begin to wake and some didn't wake at all; just quietly died. These Italians came with a tan and the patterns on their shells were lighter browns. They definitely had personalities and soon, to our immense relief, they began to lay eggs.

The Canterbury Festival coincided with a flock of those gentle October days when hawthorn berries glow in the sun while a fine mist pours slowly around the moored boats in Faversham Creek. Faversham, with its cobbled centre around the Guildhall, seemed to have largely escaped the ravages of the supermarket. The influence of the brewery was visible everywhere in the names of streets and buildings. But the powerful smell of hops and malting barley no longer dominated. The annual ritual of visiting artists' open houses was a great opportunity to see inside some old houses, some more memorable than the artwork. I was hoping to find something snail related that I might be able to sell alongside the real thing.

The first house was showing paintings inspired by the river in muted shades of grey, blue, brown and green. There was sculpture too – made from found objects: pale driftwood worn smooth by the sea, still bearing the rusty metal chains, hooks and nails of its former bondage. I admired the artwork and talked to the artist about her vision. Then there was the cottage with one room of icons glittering with gold leaf and another full of chocolate-box views of light airy Mediterranean villages painted in blinding acrylics. The cottage itself was claustrophobic: low beamed ceilings, diamond-paned windows still clutching their old uneven glass, big dark antique furniture in small spaces; walls, furniture and doorways smothered with rugs and throws and heavy tapestry hangings. When I emerged into the daylight I had to gasp in a deep breath of fresh air.

Harty Ferry is at the end of a long single track road between meadows with the occasional house. It's the place where boats used to go across to the Isle of Sheppey. Using the wooden banister rail, I pulled myself up the steep wooden stairs of the barn to the mirror at the top that reflected light into the attic studio. Hand wrought jewellery in silver and blue displayed on a white screen reflected the pale silvery blue sky. But it was the theme that caught my attention: ammonites – spiral-form fossils – like snail shells. A whole herd of beautiful pottery snails flowed across the big old table in the centre of the room, their antennae stretching up towards the skylight. I just had to have some. After a bit of haggling we came to an agreement: I would put the snails on my market stall and take commission if they sold. Even if they didn't, they ought to attract attention.

13a Cooking snails in Greece and Cyprus

A Greek student at the university in Canterbury rang me one day to say he was homesick and what he missed most was snails. With jobs so hard to find, the economy in difficulties but a good climate, Greece is said to have hundreds of commercial snail farms now exporting tons of snails all round the world. All the islands of the Mediterranean have their own way of cooking snails. But this is a Greek version that you will also find in all the places where Greek people now live.

 # Greek Snails

For 3- 4 people as a starter (mezze)

Ingredients

30 large snails

3 tablespoons sea salt

half a cup olive oil

third of a cup of red wine vinegar

one to two tablespoons rosemary

Method

Drop the cleaned snails into boiling water to blanch then run under cold water.

Remove any membranes from the lip of the shells with a sharp knife. Sprinkle the bottom of a large frying pan with the salt over a medium heat and put the snails in open side down on the salt. Cook for 1 or 2 minutes, add the oil, reduce the heat and cook for 15 minutes. Add vinegar and stir. Sprinkle rosemary over the top and reheat. Remove from the heat onto serving plates with the pan juices – serve hot.

(Some recipes suggest putting the snails into the frying pan while they are still alive but I prefer to kill them quickly first. I suspect this recipe would leave the snails rather too chewy for the English palate.)

14
Harvest Market

It was a hopper's morning: pale mist clinging to the tree trunks and clear bright sunlight on their golden leaves. The air was still cold when I left the house and tractors were out in force on the narrow lanes, trying to catch up with bringing home the wheat after a wet summer. I'd meant to pack my box of essential bits the night before but fell asleep in front of the television instead. Handouts, recipe sheets, antibacterial wipes and cloths, notebook for contacts, emergency sandwiches, bottle of water for me, spray bottle and food for the snails. I only had a dozen snails big enough to take so I put them into a clean box and loaded them last.

I was definitely late when I turned off the main road and stopped at the imposing gateway. I'd said I wouldn't stay all day but I'd cleaned out and fed the five thousand before leaving the house just in case. Along the driveway I could see a queue of assorted vehicles: muddy estate cars and battered vans alongside family cars. In the middle of it all was a red double decker playbus. Two parking attendants were talking earnestly to the driver and looking up and down. Nobody was moving and in that space I had time to remember all the things I'd forgotten to bring, like my business cards. Eventually they made a decision and walked down the row to tell us all to back out and up the lane so the playbus could turn round and go in backwards. It was already well after ten but there seemed to be no sense of urgency, so I began to relax.

It was a few years since I'd been to the manor house and the autumn scarlet of the Virginia Creeper covered more of the brickwork than I remembered. The gravel drive was covered with leaves from an avenue of chestnut trees. Freshly painted white tops on the row of oasts reflected the sun. This was a promo day for the restaurant re-opening after two years closed. A new young family had moved in with fresh ideas. Local food in season with nothing bought in precooked, I was assured. The invitation came by email. She had found my name on the Produced in Kent website and asked if I'd like to have a stall. I said I'd bring some snails along for people to see and handle if stalls were free. I didn't expect to make any money as I had little to sell except empty shells for craft work.

'We've come over from France to take over the management of the restaurant and we're hoping to be able to bring a little French influence to bear.' We were standing at the entrance to the marquee, watching the stallholders spreading out their wares.

'You might want snails on the menu then?' I looked up at her hopefully but she was looking away across the lawn.

'Oh no!' she said emphatically. 'I don't like snails.'

She looked round at the people arriving and rambled on for a moment or two about how fortunate we were with the weather before turning her attention back to me. 'What are you selling today then?'

Well, what could I say?

Stallholders greeted one another and stood around in knots discussing the day's prospects and talking up their product. I recognised a few familiar faces: the game dealer in his leather hat and apron, looking like he'd just walked out of the Australian outback, and the party plan hostess in high heels and perfect makeup. The hallway of the house started to fill with the smell of dark chocolate, ripe cheese and apple juice. The marquee smelled new and the plywood floor bounced gently when I walked across it. The food sellers did their best not to look horrified when they saw what I was carrying. Tables were laid end to end down each side and covered with sheets down to the ground. Getting round the back to reach a chair meant crawling on the floor so I decided to stay out at the front. It was easier to talk to people that way. A clown on stilts limbo-ed under the door frame and clumped around examining the goods from his great height. A small child watched his huge feet coming towards her and retreated, screaming for her mother. He waved to us all. We waved back.

By coffee time people started to drift in: young couples with toddlers in buggies and babies en papoose, grandparents holding onto grandchildren, carers with fragile men and women in wheelchairs. Families had come for the day and enjoyed sitting around chatting in the September sun. It was somewhere to take the kids that wouldn't cost an entrance fee. They were in relaxed mode, wandering and browsing but not buying much. Across the lawn, stalls were spread around the gardens under the cherry trees selling cauliflowers and plums, jams and pickles, homemade cakes, corn dollies and baskets. The stilt man turned into a magician when he came down to earth. He twisted long thin balloons into animals, swords and helmets and introduced open-mouthed children to the three card trick. He made balls appear behind their ears and pulled toy rabbits out of the hat.

In the marquee we collected quite a crowd – the snails always attract attention, even from people who are slightly repulsed. They have to come and look, even if it's only to shudder. They saunter along a row of stalls expecting all the goods to be stationary and do a double-take when they catch sight of something moving. A small elderly woman bustled into the marquee in a billow of purple sequined skirts and fringed Indian scarves, her Doc Martens sounding on the hollow floor. She stopped for a moment, looking round at the packets of fudge tied up with red ribbons, the flowery china and the pastries, earrings swinging as she turned her head. Then she saw us.

'Oh, snails! How wonderful!' she exclaimed with delight. She came straight towards me, ignoring all the other tempting delights on offer. 'Can I have a look?' I lifted one out and she offered the back of her hand as though she expected it to be kissed. She smiled at the snail, wobbling around amongst the freckles. 'Hello,' she said. 'It's nice to meet you.' The snail waved its antennae at her and tentatively tasted her skin. 'I love the feel of them, they're so cool. We used to have a big African snail in my classroom when I was a teacher. He got out one night to improve his education and ate a book about frogs.'

An earnest young man walked over to my stall slowly, frowning. He stood for quite a long time studying the snails carefully. Then he started to ask questions about how I looked after them and what you have to do before they're cooked. Finally, after he had examined the whole subject thoroughly, he came to a conclusion. 'They're supposed to be good for you, aren't they?'

I nodded. 'Indeed. Low fat and all that.'

'I've heard they've got something in them that's supposed to cure cancer.'

'Well, there are all sorts of claims,' I hedged.

'The new wonder food. Next best thing to blueberries.' He smiled with satisfaction at having found a solution and sauntered off to discover the benefits of eating fudge.

We provided a touch of the zoo that made the day for some of the children. One or two kept on coming back, cake in hand, to have another look. The little girl whose mother was selling fudge next to me was one of those. She was on eye level with the snails. I sprinkled some food on the side of the box so she could see them feeding, their little black mouths opening and closing. She seemed quite concerned when one got some food stuck on his nose and reared up as though he was trying to lick it off. She was fascinated but definitely wanted me to keep the top closed so they couldn't get out.

In the morning the marquee had seemed like a good choice of location because it offered shade for the snails. But by noon it began to get hot and a jazz band set up right behind me, which made conversation difficult. Soon after half past three the temperature suddenly dropped and we judged that no one else was likely to come. Anyone going out for the afternoon had probably already gone wherever they were going. We'd all been round and bought what we wanted from each other's stalls, counted the takings – which didn't take long – and started to pack. Parents had finished their picnics on the grass. The children had eaten what there was to eat, burst their balloons and started to fight. The snails had stuck themselves firmly into the corners of their box and refused to let go when I tried to pick them up. I shared their feelings: we'd worked hard. It was time to go home.

14a Cooking snails in Crete and Malta

Crete

Crete is another of those Mediterranean Islands that has its own traditional recipe for cooking snails usually collected from the wild.

Ingredients

Per person:

1 dozen large snails

sea salt

a small onion, finely grated

1 clove of garlic, crushed

1 large ripe tomato, chopped

a quarter cup olive oil

one cup water

half cup bulgur wheat

black pepper

chopped herbs optional

Method

Drop the snails into a large pot of boiling salted water and simmer for 15 minutes. (For personal preference I would cook them for much longer than this.) Drain and run under cold water until the water runs clean. With a sharp knife remove any membranes around the mouth of the shell; drain and set aside. In a heavy pot, sauté the onion, garlic and snails in olive oil over a medium heat, stirring frequently for 4 – 5 minutes. Fry the tomatoes then simmer covered for 10 minutes. At this stage you can add fresh or dried herbs to vary the flavour. Remove the snails and keep hot while you prepare the bulgur wheat. Stir four and a half cups of water into the pot and when steaming add the bulgur wheat and two teaspoons salt. Stir to prevent clumping then cover and cook over a low heat for 10 – 12 minutes until bulgur is soft, stirring frequently. Remove from the heat, stir in the snails and let it rest for half an hour or so before serving in soup bowls. Add black pepper to taste and chopped fresh herbs if you want them.

(Note: the visitor to Slow Summer Snail Farm who gave me this recipe prefers to use potatoes instead of bulgur wheat.)

Malta

One of my customers tells me that in Maltese markets he sees small local snails for sale everywhere. They are collected from the wild and are sold very cheaply as a good source of protein for people who may not have much money to spend. There are several species of small snail in Malta but the one that is commonly collected and eaten is the same as our common garden snail, Helix aspersa.

Snails with Aljoli

Make sure the snails are clean and well–fasted. Wash and cook the snails in salted water or sea water for at least an hour with basil and mint.

When the snails are cooked, drain them and leave them to cool for a while.

When cool, with a tooth pick pull the meat out and remove the intestines.

In the meantime prepare the aljoli - green sauce

Ingredients

For about 50 snails to serve 4 people:

4 cloves of garlic

2 tablespoons olive oil

4 tablespoons chopped parsley

1 large tomato, peeled and chopped

3 tablespoons dry bread made into crumbs

pinch of salt

freshly ground black pepper to taste

2 tablespoons lemon juice

Method

Mix all these together; cover the sauce with a layer of olive oil and then pour the sauce over the cooked snails.

This is eaten with a fork.

Some recipes add tabasco sauce or chopped tomatoes and black olives or tinned tuna fish or anchovies.

Other recipes use crushed cooked potatoes instead of bread and fry the mixture in olive oil.

15

Christmas markets

Snails don't worry about the meaning of life. They don't worship the sun but their lives are ruled by the length of the days. Holly and ivy, those symbols of fecundity, leave them cold as they slowly lose interest in laying eggs. Christmas is the lowest ebb of the year and the winter solstice is very welcome when at long last the mornings and evenings start to get lighter.

Preparing for Christmas this year was not to be about enjoying mulled wine with friends, relaxing walks across crisp snow or eating jacket potatoes around a cosy fire. Instead, I planned to spend several weeks standing outside behind a market stall trying to protect my goods from getting soaked or blown away. I had decided to try my luck with regular farmers' markets, which nearly every village and town in Kent seemed to have. In theory, it looked as though you could make a living travelling from one to the next, without the commitment and overheads of a shop.

It was early December so truncheons of brussels sprouts, mince pies and turkey with all the trimmings were everywhere. Snails were definitely off the menu. I'd been round my usual customers but no one wanted them. It was definitely time to try something new.

I watched the weather forecast anxiously each week, wondering if this time, against all the odds, it might be dry, maybe even sunny. I pitched my stall in every unsuitable place and ghastly weather imaginable: by a cliff top bandstand in a force seven, in muddy puddles and snowdrifts, outside a strip club in Soho and on a pebbly car park behind a village pub in the pouring rain.

But it wasn't just the weather that was fickle. So were the crowds that showed up to the markets that I now depended on; their decision on whether to come to the market in the first place, and their frame of mind if they did, were vital to my profit margin. Negotiating with market organisers wasn't easy either - with most I had to wait to be invited. The snails and I found it easy to get an invitation as we were offering something unique, but the fees were often high.

There was a time, when the council ran all the market sites, where the stalls went up overnight before the vans arrived, posts slotting into concrete holes in the ground. Now it's all gazebos like big umbrellas that blow about in a gale despite the weights at each corner. It takes four men to put them up and a van to carry them round. So I decided to go for something else and the idea of an old fashioned cast iron stall was quite attractive. The telescopic design meant it would fit in the back of a car and I was assured it was easy to erect and it would never blow over.

The practice run for putting it up was in the back garden on a calm sunny day, with plenty of room and no pressure. The frame slotted together neatly and it didn't seem too difficult. Spreading the heavy tarpaulin roof across it single-handed was the real struggle. People with short legs like me needed a ladder (another thing to get into the car) and if the wind was blowing it was impossible. When it went into place, it had to be pulled tight and clipped down. But the clips were two-handed jobs. There I was, wobbling about on top of the ladder, trying to hold the tarp in place and fix it at the same time, wrestling to prise open the fierce metal teeth of the clips without them snapping shut on my hand. One of the few good things about markets was the feeling of cameraderie between stallholders. We were all in it together, looked out for each other, and one of my colleagues usually came to the rescue.

Packing for markets was a major operation but there was something quite satisfying about squeezing a lot into a very small space. It was rather like doing a large heavy three-dimensional jigsaw. The frame of the stall had to go in first because of the weight – which caused problems setting up, because if it's raining you really need to put the stall up first before unpacking everything else. The list of things to take got longer each time we went to a new location, to meet the new requirements of EHOs in different towns. Some required a bowl and hot water for hand-washing even when there were public loos nearby, others wanted a first aid kit and a fire blanket. Yet another wanted a fire extinguisher and sight of my health and safety manual – and they all had to fit in the car. There were bottles of spray for the table, antibacterial gel for the hands, rubber gloves, aprons and boxes full of clean cutlery, cloths and crockery.

Finding out where my stall was supposed to be was more difficult than the early morning drive. I had to find out who was in charge and I didn't know what he or she looked like. I found myself in the middle of a noisy scrum of vans and boxes and people intent on unpacking. If I could persuade myself to ignore my rising panic as the clock ticked, eventually I might spot a scruffy unshaven man with a woolly hat pulled over his ears, big boots and a high visibility jacket, moving methodically through the melee: that was probably him. The Danny la Rue look-alike in Westville was more of a surprise, with her leopard print ensemble and blonde coiffeur. She employed a crowd of men to put up her row of matching gazebos, which we should pay her to use. She wrinkled her nose with distaste at my traditional cast iron stall.

"Oh, you've got one of those old fashioned things," she said, and she tucked us away out of sight to keep the place tidy.

At Christmas markets there were decorations in the streets. Father Christmas sometimes came on his sleigh and carol singers raised the spirits. At one event there was a crooner, like an overfed Quentin Crisp, with an electric keyboard, dyed hair and cravat to cover the scars from his facelift. He couldn't sing either and we breathed a sigh of relief when he packed up and went home for lunch.

I spent a lot of time planning how to make the stall look attractive to customers, choosing a colour scheme and finding ingenious ways to display and protect the goods. A yellow checked cloth with green and red labels in picture frames and wooden boards and bowls looked good from a distance. The picture frames helped to keep the labels dry and stop them flapping about or blowing away. I invested in a banner sporting the slogan "the ultimate slow food", with a picture of a snail crawling along it. Gold lids and labels on jars of food gave the right image for a premium product. I worried for days about how many jars of snails to make for customers to take away, or cooked ones to take to sell hot.

'Are you a snail fan?' I would shout to passers-by. It usually got me a response – but perhaps not the one I wanted.

'Have you heard the one about the snail who took off his shell because he felt a little sluggish?' I heard that joke more times than I can count.

'This is your chance to get your own back!' I told the gardeners who complained about their prize vegetables and flowers disappearing. 'Eat the little devils!'

Despite my best attempts at planning, something nearly always went wrong. At my first ever farmers' market the stall blew down in a gale. The gas for the hotplate ran out, or it was too cold for the gas to ignite, or the windshield blew away. Then, when it rained, the tarpaulin sagged and filled up, dripping over the table through minute holes that you could hardly see with the naked eye, emptying itself suddenly over the customers when a gust of wind flipped it inside out.

I usually arrived with everything except the garlic butter … or the cash box… or an apron… or the plastic tablecloth. Most of the time I didn't make enough money to cover the petrol I'd used on the journey and several times I told myself I would never do it again. But somehow there was always the thought at the back of my mind that this would be the big one. Maybe I would be spotted by an important customer who wanted to buy all my goods on a regular basis. As I stood there shivering in my boots and thermals, I imagined I could see him coming down the street with his entourage … but it was just the cold penetrating my brain. Along came another freeloader, out for a Sunday morning stroll, tasting everything and buying nothing.

To hibernate or not to hibernate, that is the question if you are a snail: whether to shut down for the winter or try to keep warm and survive till spring. In those short days and long evenings at the end of the year I struggled to ward off a sore throat, brought on by spending too much time out in the cold and wet. My head felt woolly because I wasn't sleeping well at night and couldn't keep awake during the day. When the markets finally came to an end I wrapped myself up in a blanket and fell asleep on the sofa, leaving the snails to fend for themselves.

15a Heston Blumenthal and snail porridge

Snails are a familiar feature of the menu in most Michelin starred restaurants but for one man, Heston Blumenthal, they have become a signature dish – an imaginative creation that he is well-known for. This is a version of snail porridge that is based on his recipe available on www.bbc.co.uk

Snail porridge

There are a number of elements to Heston's recipe that are cooked separately and then combined on the plate at the end with a beautiful garnish.

For the snail butter

To the usual mix of butter, garlic, fresh parsley and shallots he adds button mushrooms, Dijon mustard, parma ham and ground almonds.

For the snails

Heston cooks his snails very slowly for three hours, very much as I do (see my generic snail cooking recipe) but with additional vegetables such as celery and fennel, allowing 12 snails per person. After cooking the snails the stock is drained off and strained to use for cooking the porridge.

For the porridge

This is standard porridge oats cooked in the same stock that is used for cooking the snails.

To serve

The cooked porridge is mixed with the snail butter. The snails are sautéed in more butter and poured over the top. To garnish, fennel is thinly sliced and tossed in sherry vinegar and walnut oil. Parma ham is finely shredded and both are used as garnish on top of the porridge.

16
Egbert

On the first day of January it was bitterly cold. The sky was navy blue and snow began falling early. By mid afternoon the pond looked like an iced cake waiting for the decorator's nozzle to paint a scene. The worst snow event in twenty years, they said. The weathergirl spun new superlatives as Kent slowed down to a silent stop – schools closed, trains and buses halted, motorways seized up and the snails refused to lay. Parcels were neither collected nor delivered, but chefs were on the move.

'Could I speak to Eddie, please?'

'Who?'

'Eddie,' I said. 'Your head chef?'

'Oh, you mean that Eddie. He left ages ago.'

My heart sank. Eddie had been such a character and fun to do business with. It was Eddie who'd put 500 snails in the kitchen sink and turned the tap on to give them a good wash, then went off to do something else. Although snails enjoy a gentle shower, if they think they're going to drown they do what you or I would do and run for the high ground as fast as possible. I think it took him quite a long time to pick them off the ceiling and by then they were in galloping mode. I just hoped they hadn't eaten too much plaster.

Now, it seemed, Eddie had gone the way of all chefs and moved on when I wasn't looking. Winter was definitely a time for chefs to get restless. When business was slow, customers in short supply and not much in the way of fresh local produce to cook, they looked around for new opportunities. The snails were in the same sort of mood. They sat around in their nice warm room, sheltered from the cold winter winds and eating at my expense and didn't feel at all like putting in the effort to lay a few eggs. Why bury yourself head down in the ground concentrating for hours on end if you don't have to?

So, with Eddie gone, I spoke to Alan, who introduced himself as the Executive Chef for the hotel group.

'It's really hard to get good quality snails,' he said, 'especially live ones.' He gave me his email address so I could send some details.

The following week I rang him back to close the deal, only to be told that Alan too had left.

'But I only spoke to him Thursday! He didn't say he was leaving.'

'You're surprised?' the man who answered the phone said. 'I was working with him all day Friday and he never told me either.'

We both laughed.

So I started all over again with Jimmy, who gave me his email address and asked for information.

'You're not leaving, are you?'

He laughed. 'No, of course not!'

I wasn't hopeful.

With no money coming in, it was time for a little creative thinking – and that was when Egbert the photographic model was born. Giving the snails names always seemed like a dangerous path to go down but this was an emergency. I tried to pick something androgynous. Hermes had a certain ring to it but I thought Egbert sounded more dignified, as befits a snail who struts his stuff on the catwalk.

There were lizards and snakes on the website of the model bureau for animals but the application form was designed for cats and dogs. I made a guess for a date of birth, but gender and colour of coat required a little more imagination. The drop down box for gender gave only two options: male or female - nowhere to write hermaphrodite. So Egbert agreed he would try to pass as male, just for these purposes. For colour of coat I wrote that his shapely body was creamy white and his shell intricately decorated in gold and brown. They didn't ask for the colour of his eyes. Under further information I explained that Egbert performed well for the camera and enjoyed being handled. He also had lots of friends with different coloured shells who could come as a crowd if required. I tried to be truthful but I may have exaggerated Egbert's thespian potential just a little. The requirement for photos showed him in his true colours. I gave his shell a polish and wiped the crumbs of breakfast off his nose before we started. I could get him well lit and nicely posed looking at the camera but if I didn't click fast enough he was off, away from the lights. I couldn't get him to understand the instruction 'Stay!' It might work with dogs but not with snails. The company went to extraordinary lengths with their registration process. There was even an online pseudo interview with a smiling face on the screen asking me questions. Fortunately she didn't want to interview Egbert as he'd got tired of the whole thing by then and gone to sleep. The contract arrived by email with the demand for a large registration fee and a gagging clause. The fee was 600 times more than Egbert's commercial value on the open market so we agreed to give it a miss and he resigned himself to a reclusive life.

But Egbert had his moments of glory as a model posing for a photography project. The weather had softened by the time I came to pack him up carefully into a box marked livestock and take him to the post office. Tractors had cleared the narrow lanes where wind had blown soft snow to fill the space between the hedges. Skis and toboggans had slid back to the attic.

The counter clerk barely glanced at the box except to stick a label on it before tossing it into a sack with all the other post. I winced as Egbert sailed through the air and landed with a gentle thud. But he arrived safely and spent a week away before coming back the same way. When I unpacked him he rolled out of the box onto the table and lay still for just a moment. Then out came one cautious antenna and he looked around before he emerged, apparently unscathed, to enjoy a well earned brunch. Photos of his beautiful eyes were soon displayed on the internet for all to see.

Television was a completely different experience. Once one journalist had discovered this strange woman farming snails in her back bedroom, lots more followed. It felt as though the phone just kept on ringing with people wanting to take photos or write articles, which was all good stuff, and I kept my fingers crossed that increased sales were going to follow. It was late evening when the BBC rang me to arrange a time to come to my house the following day, which put me in a panic. I would have to get down to some serious housework if cameras were expected. I managed to get three days' grace and spent every waking hour clearing up, washing surfaces and even painting the outhouse walls, which hadn't been done for fifteen years. Some instinct made me focus on the garden, partly because it's the first thing you notice when you come in through the front door. I made a special job of the kitchen, which is the biggest space, and brought down some specimen snails of different ages hoping they wouldn't want to film in the snail room itself. It's just an ordinary room but cluttered with shelving and boxes of food and buckets. I was grateful for a sunny day so I could open the windows wide to make sure the air was fresh. As an afterthought, on the morning they were due to come, I did wipe the dust off the front door. For quite a long moment I looked at the brass knocker and letterbox, which could have done with a polish. I thought about having to unscrew them and take them off to do the job properly and decided not to bother as I'd run out of energy by then.

Paul the presenter was ten minutes early and obviously nervous. He paced up and down the kitchen and hopped from one foot to the other until he eventually asked to use the bathroom. I wondered if he wanted to check his mascara. I'd spent a long time in front of the mirror myself, trying to decide what to wear. The dress code for farmers is surely casual but I didn't want to be scruffy. I wasn't sure what colours would look best on screen and what to put on my feet. Having the right shoes is so important.

The film crew arrived on time at noon – two young women who were fascinated by the snails – so I warmed to them straight away. I steered them into the kitchen.

'We'll shoot some film in the garden but I think we should start in your spare room where the snails live,' said the producer.

'It's not very photogenic,' I warned her.

'That doesn't matter. We'll be doing close ups so no one will get any impression of the whole room itself.'

'It's full of clutter.'

'It'll be fine.'

'Wouldn't there be more space down here?'

'We'll manage,' she said cheerfully, and she started up the stairs.

They stood around on the landing and waited while I tried to clear a space. 'Can we help?'

'No thanks. I'd better do it.' I darted about trying to move things so they could get the camera in the door. I discovered all sorts of dusty treasures hidden under the table. But it was okay: when the shots appeared on screen the room didn't look as bad as I feared.

The producer wanted to film as much as possible out of doors so we had to work quickly in between showers. They spent hours focusing in with close-ups, then filmed us walking down the garden talking. Paul had a snail on his hand who he referred to as Brian, in honour of The Magic Roundabout. But before they left there was the front door scene of him leaving the house with a bag of snails to take to a chef to be cooked. Oh, if only I'd cleaned the brass!

I told Sarah to watch the local news and the phone rang as soon as it finished.

'What did you think?' I said.

'Well, it was a bit short,' she said. 'How long were they there?'

'Five hours altogether, I think.'

'That's ridiculous!'

We spent ages filming a conversation in the garden and they cut the whole thing in the end. I could only remember what I wanted to say for the first take and then found myself saying something quite different by the third and he kept forgetting his lines as well.

'But it wasn't a waste of time to get you on local TV, was it?'

'You can tell it's the silly season when a story about snails makes the news!' I said.

'I haven't seen you since you went to Belgium,' Sarah said. 'How did it go?'

Tavola Xpo had been a strange experience. The exhibition was huge and glossy, with stand after stand of men in suits propping each other up, enjoying good conversation with plenty to drink. I don't know what I expected but I felt completely disconnected. It was an alien environment. I felt like a country bumpkin and totally irrelevant. The stallholders weren't interested in passers-by at all. The most powerful message I learnt was that they weren't interested in buying English food.

I suppose they still hang onto that stereotype of the tasteless boiled meals of the past.

'The only guy who was useful was a snail caviar maker.'

'What's snail caviar?'

'Eggs … same principle as ordinary caviar.'

'What do they taste like?'

'Sort of mushroomy. They burst on your tongue … quite intriguing.'

'Easy to make?'

'He wouldn't tell me, of course … commercial secrets!'

'Of course.'

But Dominique was forthcoming about the snail market, which was really helpful. It reminded me of the visit to Pierre's farm and made me think I'd like to have a go at the French method of farming – seasonal, with the snails out of doors in the summer; when they're hibernating you get a rest. It meant I needed to find some land.

'Do you remember how Pierre's farm was open to the public?'

'Yes, we talked about that idea on the boat, didn't we? I can see you taking on too much again if you're not careful. Running a visitor attraction is a big commitment.'

'I know. I'll be careful.'

'Hmm. You forget I've known you a long time.'

'Don't worry. I'll be alright.'

16a Portuguese recipe traditionally eaten on 1 May

It's a tradition in Portugal to have snails on May 1st in celebration of Portuguese Labour Day and they are usually collected from the wild. Serve them on a large tray or in individual bowls, with an empty bowl for shells. To get the snails out of their shells use a large headed pin or tooth pick.

Collect about a kilo of small snails from the wild and starve them for 3 or 4 days to get rid of any toxic plants they may have ingested. Wash snails in running water and then place them in a large pan covered with plenty of water.

Ingredients

4 cloves garlic – crushed

the grated zest of 1/2 lemon

1 stalk fresh rosemary

2 stalks of dried oregano - with stalk and leaves

1 hot chilli pepper

Method

The traditional way to cook them is to cover the pan tightly and heat the water over a very low heat so that the snails have time to extend their heads outside the shells. On a personal note - I wouldn't kill them slowly like this because I am not convinced it is humane. Let them boil slowly for the first hour then skim, add salt and the other ingredients then simmer for another hour. The long slow cook should give you a tender meat and it gives time for the herb flavours to be absorbed. Serve warm in a small bowl, with the **cooking** liquid that you can dip bread into and eat it with the snails. You will need a small fork to pull them out of their shells.

17
Moving out of doors

The idea of farming out of doors had taken root but I needed to find a suitable space. The allotment committee had eventually offered me a patch of ground but there was pressure on space from keen gardeners so I felt a bit guilty about taking it. I also began to wonder if I really wanted to be in a more public place so I could invite people in to meet the snails. Once I started looking, I found there were empty rural business units all over the place, from redundant barns and polytunnels or wartime Nissen huts, to new steel and concrete cubes. Perhaps I should have been daunted by these signs of recession: farms that had gone out of business or families that could no longer afford to live off the land. I drove slowly round the lanes, stopping to enquire about rents and leases, space and services. Some had no water, others no source of power and many were off the main routes. But I couldn't find what I was looking for so a plea went out through the local food producers' network: 'Has anyone kind-hearted got a patch of land I could use?' Grow Plant Centre at Brogdale responded and going with them was not a difficult choice. I knew Brogdale as the place to go for fruit trees because the National Fruit Collection was growing there. But I hadn't bought a tree for ages so I needed to have a good look round to make sure it was right for us.

In my eagerness, I arrived early the next day and had time to wander round. The banner at the entrance gate trumpeted the National Fruit Collection but I could smell the blossom as soon as I opened the car door. I looked round the ample car park and ticked that off my list of desirable features. Signs pointed to the orchard trail, public toilets and information centre. A waitress was putting tables and chairs outside the café and the smell of fresh coffee and cakes drifted towards me. Behind the small group of well appointed shops in the marketplace was a sign for the rare breed pigs. Approached from behind they looked like strange shaped sheep with curly pigtails. But you could smell them before they turned round to reveal their matching piggy noses. The sheep illusion came from their woolly coats, now coated with mud from the wallow. The sign said they liked apples and they turned towards me expectantly.

'Sorry to disappoint you,' I said. They rushed up to greet me, squealing and jostling for position for a time before losing interest and wandering off when I didn't produce the goods.

Beyond the marketplace, old fashioned tin

advertisement hoardings for Pears soap and Swann Vesta caught my attention. The miniature railway ran behind a neat white picket fence complete with ticket office, signal and station platform. This was definitely a place for families.

The front of the plant centre was full of fruit trees and herbs, with free range hens scratching about in the gravel. Behind the greenhouses in front of the community allotments was a patch of ground. It was overgrown with grass and wild plants, an elder and a rampant bramble along one side, but none of that could dampen the excitement. The snails would have to be penned in to stop them raiding the allotments and keep a multitude of eager predators out, not to mention the hens. It took weeks of toil over a hot telephone to get the ground cleared and the pen complete. When it was done, the electric fence and corrugated iron made it look like a prison camp – more Alcatraz than free-range - but it was mine.

Time after time the car was filled with as many boxes of snails as it would carry and they transferred to their new home. They'd been living indoors up to then so the open air, with comparative freedom to roam, might be quite a shock. I laid paths between beds of compost and the snails went down on the ground with boxes for shade from the daytime sun. At first they galloped about exploring but their food went under the boxes each day and they soon got used to roosting there.

On Saturday May 29th the Slow @ Grow sign went up outside and we were open for business at last. Slow was a good name for a snail farm and it rhymed with Grow, the name of the plant centre. We would only be open in summer so Slow Summer Snail Farm it became. May disappeared in a flurry of activity and anxiety that blurred into the June heat like a mirage. As the sun warmed into summer my skin turned to gold. The snails clung to each other and shuffled down into the ground underneath anything they could find to catch the last remnants of moisture. The black sides of the snail pen seemed to radiate heat and we were all left gasping for rain. Those snails who didn't go in for the group hug found their own dark and secret places or climbed the walls and stuck themselves firmly down waiting for their ordeal to end. Days and weeks passed with no respite and sometimes they just dried up and died unless rescued. A sparrow flew in and couldn't find his way out. Left alone perched on top of a pallet. He looked round and eventually worked out where the door was.

I worked down the rows feeding the snails, watering the ground beneath them then covering them up with fabric to try and deflect the sun. My back was aching from bending over and I stood up and stretched before starting the last row with the youngest snails in it. I could see there were empty shells again, scattered in the dust. I'd noticed them several times and wondered if I had put the baby snails out too soon before they could stand up to the dryness. The snails hardly moved at this time of day so the rapid movement when I lifted the next box took me by surprise. I just got a glimpse of a small furry body before it disappeared into the vegetation. A mouse! It was definitely eating snails and it had to go, so I enlisted Freddie the ferret's help. I took him for a walk around the plot in his harness and lead. The first time he sniffed happily away, turning over boxes, eating cherries, drinking water out of the snails' bowls, trying to run under a piece of gutter which was full of snails and generally not being much use at all. I thought perhaps the intruder might sniff the smell of ferret and take the hint. But a few days later I was still finding empty shells.

It was several days before I saw the mouse again but this time I was better prepared. I had some netting to hand and a pair of heavy duty gardening gloves. Without the vegetation to hide in, this time he ran from one box to another so I knew where he was. I put my gloves on, lifted the box and when he ran I fell on him with hands outstretched. For a moment, as I lay there on the ground panting, I wondered if I'd squashed him but then he started to wriggle. I carefully pushed my hands together round him and ran out of the enclosure, up the path and out into the orchards to let him go. He scampered off looking quite perky considering our joint ordeal. He didn't even stop to dust himself off whereas I definitely needed a sit-down and a cup of tea to recover.

I had a feeling that wasn't going to be the end of the story. I didn't know how my rodent friend had got in so I gave Freddie a stiff talking-to and took him round again. This time he seemed to be concentrating on the job in hand and got quite excited by the scent trail he picked up round the door and along the boundary fence. I started to think the mouse, or mice if there were more, must have sneaked under the electric fence. I started the feed run with the youngest snails and soon found tell-tale signs of newly gnawed shells. There was nothing under the boxes. Then I saw an empty shell beside a water bowl and wondered if there were any more underneath the bowl. That's where I found the second mouse and this one was fatter, so I evicted her not a moment too soon. I blocked up all the smallest holes in our defences with steel wool. After that, Freddie and Dusty came with me and took up temporary residence each day. Together we spread the joyful smell of ferret around the place and they attracted just as much attention from the visitors as the snails.

Blossom still hung on the trees when the Cherry Festival came around. No sign of rain, though storms were forecast elsewhere and we held our breath as heavy rain could burst the crop. Lorry loads of fruit with pretty girls' names came out of the pack house – Celeste, Stella, Penny, Regina - I had no idea there were so many kinds. The snails and I feasted on Sunburst, Napoleon Bigareau and Amber Heart, the dark red and juicy fruit dying my teeth like Dracula's bride. I looked for signs of the snails' pale bodies turning pink too. But the snails had fussy eating habits - the waxy bright sour cherries were left scattered on the ground, their tight skins untouched.

On Festival day crowds of families lined up to take the horse-drawn dray on a trip around the orchards and filled their pockets with home-made fudge. The marquee of fruit to sample drew them in with its scent and they went away loaded with provisions. Later in the day, after they had eaten their fill, they wandered round the plant centre browsing the herbs and came across us by accident. The children swooped on the snails with delight and I took pleasure in showing them round. They were fascinated by the eggs and babies, marvelling over the size and beauty of the adult snails. I also spent a lot of time explaining what I was doing to their parents, who seemed amazed and bewildered by the whole idea. I could see there was a serious education job to do because so many people had never really looked at snails as animals worthy of study. My early training as a biology teacher resurfaced and I started to wonder if I could advertise Snail Days for children. I'd been invited to a Snail Day at Wildwood, the animal park near Herne Bay where I'd got to know Anne, the Education Officer. Lots of families had come to take part in activities centred around snails and it was a day where I felt really at home.

'You could sell those snails as pets, you know.'

I swung round at the familiar voice. 'Hello Sarah! I didn't see you coming.' Sarah had expressed another idea that was just forming in my mind.

'Couldn't you make up some sort of pack with food, perhaps, and somewhere for them to live?'

Moving out of doors had opened up all sorts of new opportunities.

17a Great British Menu, Charlie Lakin and the Marquis

Great British Menu is one of those engrossing food competitions on the BBC. Chefs from all the regions around Britain compete with one another to have their own inspired dishes selected to cook at a banquet on a special occasion. 2011 was the year when two GBM competitors chose to present dishes incorporating my snails.

Charlie Lakin, Head Chef at the Marquis at Alkham, grew up on a farm in North Yorkshire where his love of hearty rural cooking began. His career in the kitchen started before he left school and went to study catering at Yorkshire Coast College. Once qualified, Charlie was appointed Sous Chef at the Star Inn at Harome under Chef Proprietor Andrew Pern. Together they worked a modern style of cooking into old rural favourites, earning numerous awards and accolades including a coveted Michelin star. After four years at the Star Inn Charlie was appointed Head Chef at the Feversham Arms at Helmsley, a local boutique hotel. It was a great move for Charlie and the Fev'. The restaurant won numerous awards and became one of the select and exclusive Pride of Britain Hotels. During his time at the Fev' Charlie married his South African partner Paula and together they moved from North Yorkshire to the south east coast of Kent. Here he set about familiarising himself with the area and establishing the network of local suppliers and resources that are trademarks of his award-winning cuisine. At the Marquis he is the proud recipient of three AA rosettes, 4/10 in the Good Food Guide and is a rising Michelin star.

Fillet of Huss, Kentish snails, red wine and sea radish

1k large huss/dogfish tails

Ingredients

8 snails

Brine:

500ml water

35g table salt

1 strip lemon zest

1 clove garlic

1g thyme

1 bay leaf

Braising liquor:

18g shallot

1.5g garlic

6g sherry vinegar

75ml red wine

150ml double chicken stock

1g thyme

1 bay leaves

4 baby onions

18g diced celery

1 strip lemon zest

Lemon juice

chopped lemon thyme

Method

Blanch the snails in boiling water for 2 minutes to kill them; place in iced water. Using a small fork remove the flesh from the shell and discard the shells. Bring the ingredients for the brine to the boil then add the snail meat and cook for 20 mins; remove and chill. To braise the snails, sweat the shallot and garlic for 2 mins. Add the vinegar and reduce to a syrup, add the snails and red wine and cook on a gentle simmer for 30 mins. Add the chicken stock and herbs. Gently simmer for a further 1 hour or until tender. Drain the liquor into another pan to reduce it, saving a bit to reheat the snails and garnish. Reduce the braising liquor with the baby onions and celery until it lightly coats the back of a spoon. Add the lemon juice and thyme to taste and season.

Snail mince

Ingredients

4 cooked snails, coarsely chopped

5g very fine diced shallot

0.5g garlic, very finely chopped

0.5g creamed horseradish

1.5g butter

1.5g sea radish leaves, shredded finely

Method

Sweat the shallots and garlic in the butter then add the snails and horseradish, cook for 2 mins and keep warm for service. Add the sea radish at the very last moment and season.

Cauliflower puree

Ingredients

50g shaved cauliflower florets

5g butter

7.5g full fat milk

5g whipping cream

Method

Sweat the cauliflower in the butter until tender,

add the milk and cream. Bring to the boil then
puree until smooth, and season.

The Fish

Fry the fish gently in butter for a few minutes,
turning carefully.

Arrange on the plate: fish, snail mince, cauliflower
puree and whole snails to garnish.

18 Becoming a smallholder

July was relentlessly hot at Brogdale that first year. People hurried about their business in the early mornings getting in supplies, a hush descending as temperatures rose. By midday the sun beat down, drying everything it touched, cracking the clay soil and stopping seeds from germinating. I set up my festival stall beside the pen and told my story many times to anyone who came. A few visitors dropped by with promises of grandchildren to come. I spread my table and chair in the shade and opened the laptop, noticing, in the stillness, the chirp of grasshoppers nearby. Every living thing looked for somewhere shady, waiting for the sky to cloud over.

When darkness fell the stars glittered over ground that radiated heat. There wasn't a breath of wind and I tossed and turned all night. Then one morning I woke feeling refreshed and realised I had slept properly for the first time in weeks. Rain was dripping from the gutter onto the sill outside the open window, the water butt overflowing onto the path where starlings were taking an early morning bath.

As I approached the pen, I could see a couple of hens patrolling, keeping just out of range of the electric fence. Two large snails sat on the concrete path looking very pleased with themselves, unaware of the hungry beaks poised to finish them off. Somehow, they were getting under the door. I scooped them up and opened it. There were thousands of snails everywhere, marching purposefully across the ground, attacking the vegetation, climbing up the sides and hanging from the bird netting above. I picked my way carefully through and switched off the power. The first thing was to catch any escapees before they did any damage but an inspection of the outside showed just a handful of the snails were definitely mine because of course, thanks to the quenching rains, every snail in creation was out for a promenade. I grabbed one that was galloping towards tender plants on a neighbouring allotment and breathed a sigh of relief that there weren't more.

My big yellow cycling cape came into its own on days like this. I'd bought it at Glastonbury the year it rained… but doesn't it always? When I put it on I could hear the music again and remembered stamping so hard to the beat that by the end of four days my knees were swollen with the impact. Under the cape, I could work crouched down and keep dry, except where the back of my head got wet from touching the umbrella balanced across my shoulders. I fed a rows of snails, protecting the dry food as well as I could. When I got to the end of the first row, I stood up to stretch my legs and looked back to see the snails from the second row marching across the path. They were hungry. They could smell food but the service was a bit slow, so they'd decided to help themselves.

When there's water running down the hill, swirling round the potholes and roaring down the drains it feels like it has been raining forever. It was still raining when I went to Sissinghurst for the Smallholders' Fair in August.

'Look, Mum! There's the snail lady.' I was getting used to my new identity when it changed again. Without even trying I'd become a smallholder.

I had dressed for the hot sunny day that was forecast and stood in the grey drizzle in my shorts and branded vest, trying to look bright and cheerful as the tarpaulin above my head began to leak, dripping rhythmically to mark the slow passage of the afternoon. But smallholders are made of sterner stuff - we told each other we had worked in worse. The snails were ecstatically happy, of course, now the humidity was high.

'Let's have some snails. Which one would you like?' joked a father, pointing to the breeders waving their antennae at the passers-by.

His daughter recoiled in horror. 'You're not going to cook those, are you?' she asked, and everyone laughed. I reassured her that the live snails were quite safe but I don't think she believed me.

There were many farmers and entrepreneurs I hadn't met before: the hog roast, the quail farmer and the mushroom spawn vendor. The stall next to me grew acres of pick your own cottage garden flowers. Armfuls of dog daisies, sweet Williams and snap-dragons; bunches of forget-me-nots and pansies sheltered under their umbrella. They told me about the smallholder fair at Ardingly where everyone in the world of small farmers congregated to share their experiences, and I resolved to go the following year. There were heavy horses, rare breed sheep and a glamorous chocolate coloured alpaca with ridiculously long eyelashes and a coat trimmed in lines like purl and plain knitting. She gazed down at me and I desperately wanted to take her home.

Sales were good and the customers keen – it was a much bigger crowd than I'd seen elsewhere. I was selling mini snail farms for the first time and getting an encouraging response. Baby snails and everything you need to care for them went home with families looking for a low maintenance pet. Lots of people took my leaflets and thought of children in their families who would like to look after snails. This was also the right place for selling hot snails and soon the air around me was filled with the smell of garlic butter. Amateur chefs talked of rearing their own for the table and the smallholder kit began to grow in my mind: I pictured a snail house next to the chicken run in every garden. With the castle and formal gardens behind me, I stood looking out over the neat rows of vegetables and miniature fruit trees of the kitchen garden to the fields and hedges beyond and dreamed new ideas. Now that I'd started to get to grips with snail farming, maybe I could teach other people how to do it.

18a Snail pizza for Julia Bradbury

When Julia Bradbury and Countryfile came to visit the snail farm, a friend of mine made snail pizza for her and the film crew. Helen blogs as A Kentish Kitchen and joined me in wanting to make snails fit into the everyday family food that lots of people eat. Pizza is such a familiar part of our diet these days that it seemed like a really good vehicle for making snails acceptable and ordinary.

I used to think that pizzas had to be topped with tomato sauce but I've learnt that tomatoes are not essential and really you can treat them just like a hot open sandwich.

If you missed the Countryfile programme, you can watch the clip here (1 min 58 secs): http://www.bbc.co.uk/programmes/p00pzr77

To recreate the pizza, you'll need:

sufficient pizza dough to make one 12" pizza (about 165g)

100g cavolo nero, or other kale, or spinach

1 small onion, sliced finely

1 garlic clove, chopped

parma ham, to taste

Roquefort (or other blue cheese, but Roquefort melts particularly well), to taste.

3 or 4 sage leaves, fried in hot oil until crisp (this takes a matter of seconds)

as many pre-cooked snails as you like (say half a dozen per person)

rapeseed oil to drizzle over

Method

Pre-heat the oven to 230C/450F/Gas 8.

Strip the cavolo nero leaves from their stalks, and chop quite finely.

In a large pan, fry the sliced onions over a medium heat until soft and transparent, and just starting to turn brown at the edges. Add the garlic.

Add the cavolo nero to the pan, and cook until wilted – you may need to turn the pan down a little. When the kale is cooked, set the pan aside.

Roll out your pizza dough as thinly as possible. Add the kale and onion base, then all your toppings in the quantity you want them (don't go mad on the Roquefort, though – it can be overpowering).

Drizzle some oil over to finish, and put the pizza in the oven for 10-12 minutes.

When it's ready, remove it from the oven, and crumble over the fried sage leaves.

Slice and eat immediately!

19
Going to school

'The Great Snail Swap' was a gift from the BBC. Suddenly, snails were cool. The airwaves reverberated with tales of gardeners giving their common snails what they called "flying lessons" – throwing them over the fence into next door's garden - and wondering why there seemed to be just as many when they looked again the next day. Ruth Brooks, an amateur scientist, became famous on Radio 4 by turning this question into a research project. Children everywhere painted the shells of their garden snails with nail varnish and swapped with friends to test their homing instinct. In gardens up and down the land snails were labouring up fences, over walls, through hedges and maybe even across roads to find their way back to their own patch. Maybe some dallied a while on the way to nibble something delicious or greet long lost relatives. What happened when they met in the middle, we will never know. Maybe there was a "High Noon" stand off over territorial boundaries or arguments over who ate whose lunch. Maybe they just exchanged a few choice words about human behaviour. I wondered if my immigrant snails had a hankering to cross the Channel. When they climbed the walls of the pen were they heading for the A2, hoping to hitch a lift to Dover and onto a ferry?

I'd imagined the summer holidays would be full of families on a day out looking for things for children to do. But for families on holiday in Kent, the sea is probably the biggest draw. It's only when your children have satisfied their appetite for digging holes in the beach and throwing themselves into cold salty water that there is time for more intellectual pursuits. The Children's University was a wonderful concept, the dream of two visionaries who valued life outside the confines of school. The title "Learning Destination" was conferred on my snail pen, which would hopefully entice parents who saw every leisure experience as an opportunity to learn.

I'd forgotten Saturdays were for travel to a holiday destination or for returning home exhausted with a pile of dirty washing and children who've been penned up in the car beyond the point where civilisation breaks down. Then you've got to get the dog from the kennels, with all those fleas he seems to have acquired, or try and persuade the cat to return home from those neighbours who have overfed him and let him sleep on the bed. Then there's the shopping to get as everything in the fridge has turned green with age. So for the molluscs and me, weekends were often quite peaceful.

I sat at my farm gate listening to the birds. The sound of the motorway was like the sea, tyres swishing along the hot tarmac behind me. It slipped easily from my consciousness except when a siren went screaming by on a mission or motorbikes ripped up the road. Now and then I could hear a distant train, but the birds in the trees were more immediate, in the foreground of the picture. Thistledown blew from wild corners, bouncing along the gravel like tumbleweed in a Western. Dusty and Freddie were fast asleep, curled round each other in the sun.

Without moving from my seat I could see meadow-brown and tortoiseshell butterflies. A dark brown speckled hen searched diligently among the gravel for something good to eat. Someone fed the pigs an apple and I could hear them snort at each other in the fight to get it. A handful of visitors drifted by and declared themselves captivated by the snails. A puff of wind flapped the sides of the snail pen lazily like the sails of a yacht becalmed, and two peacock butterflies went dancing across the wildflower patch.

Each day the snails grew larger and eventually their shells started to turn upwards round the edge. Customers waited for the first crop of the season but it was almost the end of the school holidays before there were enough to sell.

A few days into September, I was driving along country lanes searching for village schools, the car windows wide open and sunglasses perched on the end of my nose. The snails travelled with me in a less than dignified way, snapped into maggot boxes in the boot out of the heat. Summer had made an unexpected return before the leaves had time to turn. A hoarding advertised the annual ploughing match in a few weeks' time. Stacks of empty apple boxes waited behind the hedges and my wheels bounced over conkers on the road. Signs of change showed in boarded up pubs and houses that revealed their history in their names: the Old Forge, the Penny Black, the Rising Sun. But resurrected post offices had sprouted beside village halls and new community shops in unexpected places: the snug bar of a surviving pub. Signs advertising free-range eggs and home grown fruit and vegetables reached out to grab me as I passed.

I followed the road signs of two children skipping along, to find my way to school. But I couldn't get in through the heavy metal barrier across the road. I parked the car and went up to it, looked through to the empty playground beyond and wondered how small children felt approaching these gates for the first time. I remembered my own first day at school so clearly at times like this, a time when everything was new and strange and frightening. An intercom crackled beside my ear.

'Can I help you?'

I was being watched! I looked up and smiled into the spy camera, stumbling over my words. Slowly the gates began to slide open and I ventured in, wondering if every school would have a stern receptionist to negotiate. This one was perfectly pleasant, took my proffered information and promised to pass it on. But I couldn't talk to the people I really wanted to reach.

At the next school there were gangs of workmen in paint-splashed overalls, rushing to complete redecoration, refurbishment and rebuilding. On these last few days of the holiday, teachers were in training, getting psyched up for the onslaught. School yards were sometimes full of cars but no one came to answer the bell.

In one isolated hamlet I opened the unattended gate and walked across the playground to see if anyone was there. I found an open door and called down the corridor. 'Anybody in?'

The head teacher emerged from a classroom, greeted me warmly, listened to what I had to say and invited me in. He introduced me to the handful of teachers in the staff room with the words 'I've got a snail break for you.'

I unpacked my bag and brought out the snails. A Mexican wave of revulsion swept round the table, hands thrown into the air and deep involuntary noises, when I opened the boxes and put them down.

'Ugh!'

The snails performed to perfection, heading purposefully towards a plate of fragrant biscuits as soon as they got their bearings. 'What makes you think snails have a good sense of smell?' I asked, and my audience leaned forward. I had their attention.

It was a long time since I'd served my apprenticeship in the classroom. I taught in the days when the boys wore caps on their heads and touched them deferentially if we met in the street, with a polite 'Good morning, Miss.' I was always 'Miss' even though I was married and, for a whole year, the only woman on the staff apart from the school secretary and the lab technician. For a long time afterwards, I had nightmares about the trials of the classroom: boys who were bigger than me and had no intention of doing anything I said. They were used to being "slippered" on their backsides for misdemeanours and the Head boasted that caning them was good for his golf swing. I could hardly engage in such physical punishment, with its sexual overtones. I wasn't much older than they were and some boys begged me to keep them in after school, so detention was no deterrent either. I hope they managed to emerge from the experience less damaged than I did.

The following day I was on the road again. One of my tyres was soft from hitting too many potholes, so I went over the speed bumps very slowly. The roads through the housing estate were narrow, with cars parked on both sides, and my heart sank as I turned into the entrance to the school. The railings were at least ten foot high round the collection of prefabricated white boxes that made up the school and there was an intercom between me and the car park again.

'I'm here for a meeting of Extended Schools Coordinators,' I said in response to the woman's voice wishing me a good morning from the grille on the post. The gates swung open towards me very slowly and I drove in cautiously in case there were more traps for the unwary inside. I half expected a pit to open up and swallow me.

Fortunately for people like me with knowledge to sell, primary schools were tasked with encouraging children to take part in what were called "meaningful activities" outside school hours. I judged that learning about snails was very meaningful and I was sure the children would agree with me. All I had to do was persuade the teachers.

I had to show photo ID to get through reception and have a visitor's label stuck to my coat. I was chaperoned down the warren of corridors to the meeting room and out came my willing performers onto a new stage. There weren't any biscuits this time but the desk was piled with papers to explore. Apparently the agenda tasted good.

I fielded questions about how they were cooked and the usual one about their names and whether I had a favourite.

'I think I'm bonding with this one,' said a teacher who looked like a schoolboy himself with his waxed hair standing up above his branded sweatshirt. 'Do you think he will know me if we meet again?' He put his head down so they were eye to eye and smiled. 'We used to have African land snails but they got a bit out of hand.'

'They have a nasty habit of laying thousands of eggs,' I agreed.

'One of the children took them home for the holidays and her mother let them go in the garden when she got fed up with having them around. A few months later it was on the news that something was eating all the vegetation along a stretch of the Royal Military Canal. I wasn't surprised when they found out what it was. Those snails could eat for England.'

'Did you own up?'

'What do you think? The bill for the eradication wasn't coming out of my budget.'

The chairman called the meeting to order and the proceedings began, with me retrieving snails from time to time when they got too close to the edge of the table or threatened to engage an unwilling guest in audience participation.

That was the start of my excursions into classrooms, much to the delight of children and amazement of teachers. I introduced myself as a farmer and tailored my approach to the topic in hand, which varied from mini-beasts to environment week to Bastille Day. It was exhausting answering the same questions and explaining myself over and over again. The snails began each day looking bright and exploring small hands with enthusiasm. They gradually lost interest as the day wore on and we worked our way from class to excited class. By two o'clock they'd shut up shop and refused to cooperate at all. I wore out at about the same speed and by the time I'd repeated myself eight times I couldn't remember what I'd said and what I hadn't. But at the end of it all, it was good to leave with a cheque and their thanks.

'That was the best day we've had in ages,' said one earnest lad of about six.

Sometimes the snails went on holiday without me. A clutch of baby snails travelled to Wales for sixth formers to look after as part of their course. They were cared for and cosseted; given all sorts of different kinds of food, then carefully weighed each day. The girls brought titbits from home to tempt them; grew cress and bean sprouts to enrich their environment, as the curriculum called it. Their behaviour was observed and every move recorded. At the end of term the girls gave them a last supper and a good drink, then they came back home, courtesy of Royal Mail.

The snail fan club was growing.

19a Worldwide market for snails

Snails are on the menu all around the world, not just in Western and Eastern Europe. I've heard snail stories from Singapore, Malaysia and Korea, Australia, New Zealand, South America and the USA. I've been asked for advice by would-be farmers in Japan, Canada and the USA but often been unable to help because of the strict import rules. There are snail farms in most of these countries but in the USA and Australia, for example, there are tough interstate rules on transporting live animals as well as import bans. So the market is definitely there, but the local farmers are protected because it is sometimes difficult for European would-be importers to access markets outside Europe.

Antipasti of snails

Blanch, de-shell and cook the snails in well flavoured stock for at least an hour and a half.

Dry the snails and pack them in sterilised jars.

Mix equal quantities of good quality rapeseed oil and cider vinegar and pour into the jars.

Use 4 cloves garlic in every half pint of oil and vinegar dressing;

salt and pepper to taste;

plenty of fresh thyme.

Remove the air bubbles with a spatula and seal carefully – you could do this in the oven the same way as you seal jam jars but the oil and vinegar may go cloudy when heated.

Keep 4 – 5 days in the fridge before using.

Should keep unopened for one year.

Eat within one month after opening.

(Thanks to Anne at Clews Pickles)

A Mallorcan recipe given to me by A Kentish Kitchen

Sobrasada is a soft Mallorcan sausage, like pate and flavoured with paprika to give it a deep red colour. You could make your own English version of pork pate but don't forget the paprika!

Mash seasoned potatoes with some sobrasada sausage, allowing one small potato per person and about half an inch of sausage. The mash should be pink and the exact amounts will need to be adjusted to taste. Spoon the mash onto a small plate and pour over it at the point of serving, cooked snails in garlic and herb butter.

Sweet potato can be used instead of ordinary potatoes if you prefer.

20

Hibernation

Rebecca came down for the cider festival in September to help me cook and bottle snails for sale. It was good to have time to talk and made festival days easier to manage. Saturday dawned bright but the hot summer faded into a memory in the cool gusty wind that lifted our market stall from the ground. Groups of friends stood around the entrance to the cider barn, hugging glasses to them closely, wrapped in the warm sounds of the band and each others' conversation. Sunday was grey and wet and few people came, so we all retreated indoors early.

The wind covered the lawn with autumn colours laid out like a carpet and I returned from walks with pockets full of sweet chestnuts to roast. Birds, suddenly exposed by the nudity of the trees, swung like high wire acrobats from tree to pond and back up to rooftop, their activity creating a feeling of excitement and anticipation. Clouds of bright leaves billowed along the gutter, gathering sweetie wrappers and small children on their way to school. My garden was overgrown with long grass and weeds galore from a season of neglect. Suckers sprouted a forest round the greengage tree but there were still ripe raspberries for tea. The ivy had grown up as far as the bathroom window. With nesting birds long gone I could trim it back, leaving the flowers heavy with pollen for late flying bees.

In the afternoon gloom in my garden I could see the

outline of two well-rounded furry bodies stretched up at the wire of their cage, looking out for supper. Freddie turned a delicate shade of apricot as his thick winter coat came through. The colour reminded me of the days when women dyed their poodles to match their frocks. Dusty looked even more like a small panda, with her plumped-out body and the circles of dark fur round her bright eyes. Their feet felt cold when I picked them up to take them indoors for some exercise. They chased each other round the kitchen floor and fought over a plastic bag, climbed my legs and begged for scraps of the vegetables I was peeling, running off with each piece to eat it in secret or squirrel it away in the cupboard under the sink. When I opened the cupboard later I would find the pegs tipped out of their box and replaced with a neat row of strips of cabbage stalk. In cold weather I might give them an egg as a treat. At least they couldn't run off with that and hide it.

They slept in a nest made of an old fleece jacket, which needed washing regularly as they didn't clean their feet before getting into bed. When the weather was wet and they looked muddy I tried bathing them but they were not at all keen on soap and water, defending their bodies vigorously with tooth and claw. I also had to change their fleece for a clean one, but each time they were suspicious of this foreign object that didn't smell right and dragged it out of the nest box, leaving it on the ground outside. Sometimes I had to put it back several times before they would admit defeat. When I picked Dusty up under her shoulders, she braced her front paws against my fingers and held herself up. Freddie, by contrast, went floppy, like a protester lying in the path of progress. When I picked him up his body relaxed, front paws loose in their sockets as he slid down slowly through my hand.

The Apple Festival was the last and biggest event of the year, when the orchards truly became the star of the show.

The marquee was filled with the sharp smell of ripe apples and pears in every shape, colour and flavour to taste and buy. The band played as we danced on the spot to keep warm and two gleaming shire horses pulled visitors round to see the crop. My stall enticed people in with the smell of hot garlic butter and the chance to adopt a snail. I met a lot of people who were tired of the rat race. It's that feeling that comes over you when you realise you've been sold a pup: the job and reliable pension you had to trade in your soul to get and keep ends up deserting you when times grow hard. Those who had lost their way and were wondering where they had gone wrong in drawing up their priorities gravitated to my door. There was an engineer who drove all the way from Hampshire without checking first that I would be there. He'd decided to take redundancy and was looking at the options to find an alternative way of making a living. A couple from Norfolk dropped by on their way to France on holiday and told me their tale. They were breeding wild snails in a cold frame in their garden to sell to Portuguese farm workers who had come as seasonal pickers. There was the couple from Shropshire who were going to build their own house in Tunisia and were thinking about setting up a snail farm there. The desire to till the soil seemed to be very strong. Animals in general are so much nicer than people and snails in particular are undemanding. They don't appraise your performance, require you to meet deadlines, clock in early or work late, become a slave to technology, up-skill or downsize. They will happily go on munching their way through their peaceable lives at a hypnotic pace, barely noticing whether you are there or not. Any rods that you make for your own back are entirely self-inflicted.

After it was all over and the last car had driven out of the gate it was time to close and put the summer to bed.

Collecting snails and taking them indoors to hibernate became a daily task as autumn drew on. After each visit I returned home with as many crates as my little car could carry. In the third week in October the weather station at Brogdale registered minus three; the snails were barely feeding at all and the task became more urgent. Every time I thought I had found the last one I found more. I cleared away the vegetation and found fugitives hiding in nooks and crannies. There were snails sleeping everywhere: stuck under leaves, tucked under stones, behind wooden posts and dozens packed into an abandoned blackbird's nest.

Soon the rustling stack of crates in the shed almost reached the roof. We were all set for winter; harvest gathered in. But outside it turned mild and started to rain. It was hardly even cool at night, and 17 degrees by day. The shed creaked with activity in the late afternoon and early evening just after dark. When I opened the door a forest of antennae waved to me, looking out for their dinner. There was definitely a bit of a rebellion brewing. One warm late evening I felt the need to look in on them before I went to bed. I took my torch to check and against the white wall I picked out the silhouette of a mass break out. An advance party of intrepid explorers climbed the himalaya of crates, cheered on by their friends and relations as they went. Somehow they had chewed through the string closing the nets they were in and found their way out.

But the following day, stepping out of the back door into the evening air, I felt a chill and looked up at a clear starry sky. The Indian summer was coming to an end. The snails, curled up in their shells, felt cold to the touch and I hoped they would survive.

On my last visit to Brogdale to clear out the debris of the year, I had to knock ice from the water bowls and prise the last hidden snails out of the grasp of frozen soil. There was a cold wind blowing dark clouds across the sky as I switched off the electric fence. But as I walked away, with the snails tucked up for the winter, I was already thinking forward to spring. I had started this adventure to realise a dream but the snails had gently drawn me in and I was firmly caught in their silvery trail.

20a Summary of cooking with snails

To put snails into context, let's look at the range of edible molluscs available first. There are not many poisonous molluscs and eating seafood is well-established. Cockles and mussels, winkles and clams, oysters, cuttlefish and squid are all eaten in Britain. There is a vast range of other sea specialities that are also good to eat but are seen on the menu here more rarely – for example razor shells and limpets. Their food value is undisputed as a source of protein and essential vitamins and minerals. Although shellfish are generally low in fat, the small amount of fat they do contain is beneficial, notably Omega-3 fatty acids that are thought to play a protective role against heart disease and aid memory and concentration. Seafood is generally cooked rapidly and does not benefit from longer time on the heat.

The general points to remember when cooking snails are as follows:

Snails are the ultimate slow food - they need cooking slowly to get a good texture. The longer and slower you cook them the better. I know a chef who puts them into a water bath at 70 degrees for 4 hours. You should aim for a soft texture like mushrooms.

There seems to be a debate about whether or not you need to remove the liver or the intestines in general. Some chefs remove some parts and others don't.

Some recipes suggest heating the live snail slowly but I am not convinced this is humane and prefer to kill them quickly. You can do this either with boiling water or by freezing but I found it more difficult to remove the snail from the shell when they had been killed by freezing.

They can be cooked in the shell or out of the shell but again I found it more difficult to remove the snail from the shell if they were cooked in the shell. You need to do that if you want to stuff the shell e.g. with garlic butter before serving. On the other hand, if you want to serve them in the original shell for the diner to enjoy the ceremony of removing them from the shell then that's a different matter.

My preference is to kill the snails by dropping them into boiling water, then removing the meat from the shell before cooking. With farmed snails the shells seem to be more fragile than wild ones – perhaps because they grow so quickly. That means the shell may break during cooking and you could end up with bits of shell in your meal.

Most people want to remove the slime before cooking though I have never understood the obsession with slime. Personally I don't think snails are particularly slimy. But boiling in brine and rinsing with good quality vinegar should do the trick.

The flavour you add in your cooking liquor is vitally important. According to Elizabeth David's "French Provincial Cooking", snails taste of whatever you cook them in. I disagree slightly because I think snails do have their own flavour and I always compare them with mushrooms, in flavour as well as texture. However, the quality of your cooking liquor can make a huge difference.

Serving suggestions

In certain parts of the world snails are street food or a snack. At a restaurant or supper party, snails mainly seem to feature as a canapé or hors d'oeuvre/antipasti but they can also be part of a fish or meat course, either as a principal ingredient, e.g. Heston Blumenthal's famous snail porridge or as a garnish. They can also form a dish in Spain's well know tapas selection. So far I haven't come across any suggestion that they could appear further down the menu, perhaps as a savoury.

Starters/ canapes

Chop the cooked snails into garlic and herb butter and serve hot or cold on small rounds of French bread.

Make mini pies with shortcrust pastry stuffed with mushrooms and chopped cooked snails with herbs.

Main courses

Serve cooked snails on skewers wrapped in bacon and sage leaves and rolled in herbed breadcrumbs.

Pour cooked snails in garlic and herb butter over a bed of lentils.

Stuff flat mushrooms with chopped cooked snails and garlic and herb butter.

Make or buy your favourite tomato based pasta sauce, add cooked snails and serve with pasta.

Use cooked snails in a wine sauce as a garnish for white fish or salmon.

Add snails to a beef stew in the way that oysters used to be used in the past.

Garnish a green salad with cooked chopped snails mixed with crumbled crisp bacon.

Give a lift to a hearty thick vegetable soup by adding cooked snails.

End Notes

Produced in Kent

Produced in Kent is a membership organisation dedicated to championing local food, drink, products and services in Kent. Its role is to promote local and seasonal produce and provide support and services for Kent businesses in the food, drink and artisan craft sectors.

For small food producers such as myself this organisation, the knowledgeable staff and its generous members are vitally important.

Canterbury Archaeological Trust

The Trust was my main source of information about the influence of the Romans on the food of local people in East Kent 2,000 years ago.

The Canterbury Archaeological Trust was formed in 1975 to undertake excavations, research, publication and the presentation of the results of its work to the public.

Grow at Brogdale

Grow specialist plant centre at Brogdale Farm is the place to go for fruit trees from the National Fruit Collection and food plants for people who want to grow their own fruit, herbs and vegetables. www.brogdaleonline.co.uk

Brogdale Collections is the home of the National Fruit Collection www.brogdalecollections.co.uk

Brogdale Market Place for Tiddley Pomme, Courtyard

Restaurant, Flowerart, Brogdale Cottage Foods, Country Practice, the Butcher at Brogdale and more: www.brogdalecollections.co.uk/marketplace/index.html

Conchological Society

www.conchsoc.org/ for people with a general interest in molluscs.

Malacological Society

www.malacsoc.org.uk/ for research papers on molluscs

Isituto Helicicultura, The National Snail Breeding Institute, Cherasco, Italy

http://www.lumache-elici.com/

Other sources of information

Bailey, Elisabeth Tova, (2010) *The Sound of a Wild Snail Eating*, Green Books

Brooks, Ruth, (2013) *A Slow Passion: snails, my garden and me*, Bloomsbury Publishing

Cameron, R. illustrated by Gordon Riley (2008) *Land Snails in the British Isles*, Field Studies Council; an AIDGAP publication

Cloudsley-Thompson, JL. & Sankey, J. (1961). *Land Invertebrates - a guide to British worms, molluscs and arthropods (excluding insects)*, Methuen & Co. Ltd, London.

Kerney, M.P. and Cameron, R.A.D. (1979) *A Field Guide To The Land Snails of Britain and North-West Europe*, Collins, London

The Food Standards Agency http://www.food.gov.uk/

The Old Foodie http://www.theoldfoodie.com

Acknowledgements

The process of setting up and running the snail farm and writing this book alongside it has been lengthy and fraught with difficulties. I would like to thank all those who have offered support and encouragement along the way. Produced in Kent and all its members deserve star billing in providing support to small struggling food producers. Canterbury City Council and Natalia Sukhram have also supported me in my business venture. There's always been someone to talk to when the going got tough. I've taken advantage of the support of writing groups too and particular thanks go to Medway Mermaids, Nanowrimo members in Kent, Nikki Chesterman, John Stewart and everyone who has patiently listened to my obsession with snails.

Thanks to Janet at The Old Foodie (www.theoldfoodie.com) for permission to reprint some old recipes. Thanks for invaluable help with editing and shaping the book go to Philippa Moore at Cornerstones; preparing the book for publication, Alison Neale at the Proof Fairy and Jane Dixon-Smith at JD Smith - Design.

Printed in May 2021
by Rotomail Italia S.p.A., Vignate (MI) - Italy